A Tale
OF Spirit

Yours, Mine and Lessons from the Universe

To Adele,
May you continue to
follow your own star of
peace, light, and Joy!
Doris Mae Honer

A Tale
OF *Spirit*

Yours, Mine and Lessons from the Universe

DORIS MAE HONER

Outskirts Press, Inc.
Denver, Colorado

Acknowledgements

Grateful thanks are extended to the two writer's group I attend regularly, one in Tucson, Arizona, and one in Victoria, B.C. To Joyce Hodges for forming the group in Tucson, to Virginia Quarels for her gentle critiques, to Francine Atkins for her inspiration, Julie Bonser for her down-to-earth assessments, and Jeanne Moore for her fabulous way with words. In Victoria, B.C. I express thanks and great appreciation to the Gordon United Church writers, Shirley Barrett, Carmen Comrie, Agnes and Gordon Craig. They bring a whole new dimension of honesty and helpful critiques from their Canadian viewpoints. In both groups we have enjoyed growth and sharing in our writing. I know readers of A Tale of Spirit will take pleasure in reading a few stories from both writers' groups which are included in this book. Another writer, Louise Rose, is a well loved and respected friend of many years. Her story of Charles and Spirit is both heart wrenching, but beautiful in its closure.

A loving thank you to my sister, Margaret, who believes in me and has always encouraged me to continue to write and to follow my own star.

Sir Isaac Newton wrote, "If I have seen further it is by standing on the shoulders of giants."

One of my giants, Michael Williams, has helped me realize my dream in writing. In the descriptive words of Dan Rather(The Speakers Sourcebook)..."The dream begins with a teacher who believes in you, who tugs and pushes and leads you to the next plateau, sometimes poking you with a sharp stick called truth." Michael Williams is that teacher.

More giants are the Canadian medical specialists who have kept me in tune, as well as the "Back to Back" healers (Drs. Rabnett and Morrison) who have enlarged my knowledge of the body's need for balance, and helped me go inwards, where my real healing began.

Another giant is Dr. Gregory Porter, who has cared for my family since 1996. He is an excellent doctor of internal medicine, as well as a philosopher, comic and friend. To him, the world of medicine includes both the science of medicine, a respect for other healing modalities, plus the world of hope and belief. I thank him for his insights into the strengths and weaknesses of the US health-insurance system and for his care of me so that I continue to live and to write.

My parents and grandparents were pioneer giants who helped open one Canadian province and who mattered very much to their communities. They taught strong values, a respect for God, Spirit and life, and a belief that we can all attain our dreams if we work towards their realization.

Thanks to Outskirts Press in the USA for their help in bringing me through the process of publishing, and to their fabulous artists.

Lastly, I give a big thank you to my grandchildren, especially to granddaughter, Hope. It was because of her insistence that this book has been written.

Contents

Introduction:

When I worked in a facility giving care to those chronically ill, I noticed that the elders loved to reminisce. Their stories were told over and over, and it is sad that their legends and history died with them.

Throughout my life I have met people who shared their thoughts and experiences with me once they found me trustworthy. All of them at one time or another express much relief that their experiences are respected and acknowledged, where, and I quote them, "Most people would say I am crazy!" Their experiences are real. So are mine. Spiritual experiences have been acknowledged since time began, are mentioned often in the bible, and are known without question by our indigenous people. I often wonder what made our present population so sure that the wonders and experiences of Spirit should be called "crazy."It was with surprise and joy that I discovered an author, Fern Michaels, in her book "Lethal Justice," writing about one of her heroines, the lawyer Nikki, whose daughter Barbara came to talk to her in spirit form. She explains that a person has to be open, in order to receive communication from the other side.

Everyone has the ability within themselves to feel and have Spiritual experiences, but some people are more developed in this way, than others. Children are wonderful at hearing and seeing the Spirit. I'm writing A Tale of Spirit with all the truths of Spirit, and hope the many others out there will gather courage to share their experiences too. God lives and Spirit is His/Her gift to us.

This is a collection of life stories which come from oral family history passed down to me, as well as anecdotes from other people's lives. Included within are my own personal experiences also. There is no particular order in terms of time, so you can hop from one story to another whenever you like. The quotes are thoughts from my favorite authors as well as thoughts I've written in my journal through the years.

The thread of Spirit runs through all our lives in many different ways, keeping us attached to the real reasons we chose to come here. In my earlier life, I took up painting, both in oil and acrylics, and I see emotions and Spirit in color. In all the stories gathered, you may notice that emotions and Spirit are sometimes woven through different situations in strong red, blue, green, gold and purple colors, the many shades of love, wisdom, beauty, trials and peace. The stories also bounce with a little history of how life was lived in the "old days" as my Grandson Jared would put it. In my book I talk quite a bit about "the old days", how things were in the time and place where I grew up.

I might have called this book by a different name, but I believe there is Spirit in all things, nature, culture, choices, people, situations, because in the biggest scheme of things, I find we are never alone, and Spirit is with us, a part of us, since the time of creation. We simply must keep ourselves open to Spirit.

I've learned from any tragedy or chaos, the order of the Universe will always emerge. The tragedies become vehicles of growth for us.

My personal history includes being a registered nurse for thirty-five years, my specialties were Neurology, Psychiatry and Obstetrics. After that career I went back to school obtained diplomas in Recreation for special populations, another diploma in Gerontology. I opened my own business, taught Gerontology in Northern College, in Kirkland Lake, Ontario, Canada, and expanded further by continuing my education to obtain a degree, with a major in recreational arts. I also opened my own business, brought music, art, puppetry and writing into different facilities, some for the aged, others for the mentally handicapped or physically disabled. In Kirkland Lake I wrote a column in a local newspaper, the Northern Daily News. My column was about the local folks there, giving them credit for their work, as well as for themselves. My first marriage was to a nice Peruvian man who spoke little English when he came to Canada. I coached him in English and he taught me Spanish. As he learned more English his courses became more clear and he achieved his Bachelors in Commerce. We both worked, saved, bought our home and raised our family, three amazing children. We grew apart and divorced after the children left home to start their own careers. My new beginning gave me freedom to explore on a deeper level my own life and my Spirit. My second marriage was to a wonderful man named Bryan who struggled with chronic illnesses, became ill and died too early. His spiritual experiences are included in my book. Later I married Ray, my present husband in 2000, and we enjoy great, gentle happiness together. Writing has been one of my passions since a very young child, especially poetry and short stories.

Bright dreams are different from usual dreams in my life. I have received bright dreams (called visions) since early childhood and they never fail to fill me with a sense of wonder. These are mentioned periodically in my book, since they have answered so many of my questions, and given me positive direction.

I like to think of life as climbing mountains, crossing the plains, descending into valleys and learning all the enriching lessons of the journey. Certainly, like everyone, I have made mistakes, fallen off mountains, and done my share of weeping, but through it all, one fact shines brilliantly, like the star of Bethlehem. We are never alone.

CHAPTER 1

The Valiant Spirit of Northern Women

We learn that love is imperative and that fear is to be transposed into positive action - DorisMae Honer

Laura Honer was frantic. Her five-month-old baby, Patricia, was gasping for breath and had been going into paroxysms of coughing. Laura was beside herself with worry and fatigue, having been up with her baby day and night since the baby became ill.

It was in the small mining community of Kirkland Lake in northern Ontario and the year was 1930. A cold November wind was howling, wildly whipping the snow outside, reducing visibility to almost zero. More and more snow was falling. Taxi drivers were refusing to drive up the hill where Laura lived for fear of getting stuck.

Suddenly, there was a knock on the door. Laura threw another blanket over the quivering, struggling baby in her arms, and went to answer. When she opened the door, she gasped in amazement and thankfulness.

Catherine Lamb, her mother, stood in the doorway.

"I just knew I had to come," Catherine said as she entered the home, slamming the door against the wind. She shook her coat and stamped her boots, sending snow everywhere.

"But, but, how did you know?" Laura gasped.

"I just knew," Catherine said again, her intense blue eyes quickly examining Patricia's trembling body as the baby heaved in almost a convulsion before still another exhausting cough.

"Its whooping cough," Catherine muttered after hearing the sound of the baby's cough. "We have a lot of work to do, so let's get busy."

Catherine explained that she had "prayed the train" from New Liskeard to Swastika, an even smaller town about 10 miles from Kirkland Lake. From there, she had "implored God" to at least get the taxi to the bottom of the hill. From there, bag in hand - she had trudged the long distance up to Laura's door.

"Walking up that hill through the deep snow took some doing," she said, "but I'm here!"

(Catherine Burnett was born in Hurdville, McKellar County, outside of Parry Sound, Ontario, Canada, on December 4, 1880, and had been the third child in a family of seven children. In fact, she was taken out of school in Grade 3 to help raise her brothers.

Later, when she had her own family, she insisted that each of her daughters receive a good education, something she had been denied.

When Catherine was in her teens, she apprenticed with the local seamstress. She married Albert Absolom Lamb in Parry Sound and the newlyweds traveled by train and boat to New Liskeard, a little more than 50 miles southeast of Swastika.

For the trip, Catherine had made her own stylish suit, the traveling clothes she would put on after the wedding. Her skirt was fashionably long. When she stepped off the horse-drawn carriage in front of the home Albert had constructed for them, she stepped into a foot of mud. It had been raining for weeks and the gravel roads had turned to liquid earth.

Catherine had long black hair tied up in a bun and her cornflower blue eyes never missed a detail. She had a quiet, purposeful way about her which endeared her to all who knew her. She was a woman who could be counted on.

There was only one doctor in New Liskeard and it seemed inevitable that Catherine would come to his attention. She had *stitched up a horrible gash in her husband, Albert's, leg, where a long saw had cut him. He was working as a lumberman at the time.*

She had kept the wound free of infection with herbs and poultices, and when the doctor saw her beautiful stitching of that long wound, he was amazed. He asked Catherine to assist him. As a teen, Catherine had learned to deliver babies and how to use the various herbs and remedies taught her by her pioneer grandmother, who had been taught folkloric medicine from the native peoples.

Sometimes she would work with the town doctor long into the night operating on some emergency case. It was a pioneer time and people just did what they could with the resources available.

Catherine became known and trusted in her community. But she was also known for something extraordinary.

For example, she would often interrupt preparations for supper, or bathing the children, and start preparing for an emergency situation. She would put a basin of water and the old flat iron on the black iron stove to heat them, and then she would start ironing the sheets she kept stored for "medical use" so as to sterilize them.

From a special drawer would come her case, holding a particular curved needle, and she would thread it and drop it into boiling water. There was no phone line at that time. Shortly after she was ready, there would be a knock at the door.

Outside there might be one man or several carrying a pain-ravaged fellow worker.

"Just put him on the couch there," Catherine would calmly say, "and wait while I wash my hands."

She then would work on the wounded man until she had cleansed, disinfected and stitched the wound. Sometimes the men had to hold their mate down while she worked, but they trusted her, and she was able to start the healing process.

How did she know people were coming for her help? Catherine Burnett Lamb was psychic.

(Catherine Burnett Lamb was also my grandmother. Laura Honer was my mother and baby Patricia, one of my sisters.)

Quickly, Laura and Catherine prepared the room for baby Patricia with steaming kettles, set on the tiny electric stove which dad had brought from the Lake Shore mine's electric shop. Dad was the chief electrical superintendent for the company.

Steam soon permeated the tiny room where Patricia lay in her crib and the baby finally began to relax. Catherine then began applying poultices of oatmeal and mustard and wet moldy bread.

Later, she cleansed Patricia with a solution of Epsom salts and water. Thanks to my grandmother, Patricia Maureen Honer survived the whooping cough, surprising even the local doctor.

Patricia grew up to be a kindergarten specialist and married Gordon Littlejohn, a mining engineer who later became a lawyer. They had three children.

Her son, Mark, was mentally challenged and died at age 11. Patricia started a tiny school for mentally challenged children and the school blossomed into a very large learning facility and a teaching centre for caregivers. Her daughter, Maureen, received her Master's diploma in journalism, and is a freelance writer for several different magazines. Her son, Bruce, followed in his father's footsteps and became a lawyer.

Patricia Honer Littlejohn and her husband, Gordon, were responsible for giving many valuable gifts to mankind. Patricia died at 72. During her precious lifetime she accomplished many good works.

I still remember the first time I went on a train ride with my grandmother, Catherine. She was taking me down to New Liskeard to meet my grand-dad. I was just over three years of age at the time and the year was 1937. My granny had come north by train to visit our family and to retrieve me, and we headed back south.

We had been enjoying the trip back together, when the conductor came walking down the aisle of the train asking loudly: "Is there a doctor on board?"

The second time he came into our train car, my grandma stopped him, and asked what the problem was. After quietly conferring with the conductor a few moments, she turned to me and said: "This man is the conductor. I've asked him to take care of you because they need me in another car. Someone needs my help." She hurried away into the next train car.

The conductor scooped me up and hoisted me onto his shoulders. He also gave me his conductor's cap to wear and took me around the train. I met many nice people on the train, including the coal-blackened men who were shoveling coal into the furnace at the front of the train.

I wanted to blow the train's whistle and they let me. I was allowed to grab that lever and, with all the strength of a three year old - and maybe a little help from the train's engineer - I heard the power of that whistle. What a wonderful time I had while waiting for my granny.

When we got to grand-dad's in New Liskeard I overheard my grandmother telling him that she had helped a lady who was in labor and had helped deliver a baby boy in the train's ladies' room.

At granny and grand-dad's place, there was a big, black iron stove in the kitchen and one electric light bulb hanging from the ceiling. A fly catcher also hung from the ceiling and curled down like taffy, with several flies attached to it.

There was one tap connected by hoses to a nearby spring and it gave the coldest, sweetest-tasting water. In the living room, there was a pot-bellied stove which heated the main floor of the house. A pipe went through the ceiling and heated the upstairs to a lesser degree.

Granny used to put a stack of hot newspapers or department-store catalogues - which she had heated at the back of the wood stove - into our beds to warm them for us before we slept. There were linoleum floor coverings throughout the house. In the entrance, ascending to the upper floor was a wonderful cherry colored set of stairs with a banister which provided good sliding for us grandchildren.

I spent many summers at my grandparents' house when I was

young. I'd like to tell you a bit about my grand-dad, because he was unique.

My grand-dad Lamb was born in St. Mary's, Southern Ontario and was brought north, on the shoulders of his Dad to Huntsville, Ontario when they literally opened up the North on foot. They were pioneers. Grand-dad Lamb worked in Magnetewan, Ontario, as a forestry helper, and guide for hunters. He had learned the native Canadian dialects and helped teach the local tribes to read, write and do simple arithmetic. Later he worked as a lumber jack, and was also good with his hands, a carpenter and a man of all trades. The native Canadian peoples respected and accepted him in all the many tribes along Lake Superior, and other regions where he travelled. He was blonde, slim, and had a mustache, under high cheekbones. His eyebrows were a bit bushy over very twinkling blue eyes. He had lost some of his teeth. Apparently they had become infected and he pulled them out with a pair of pliers. Grand-dad gave respect to all people, and expected the same in return at all times.

His hands were large and gnarled, strong from working all trades where he used his hands and body. No job was too tough or too menial for him. He believed in working hard, and believed people should take care of themselves. He refused what he called "the government's hand- outs" which were the unemployment and old age pensions. He said, "hand- outs make people soft and dependent."

When my grand-dad became ill I helped granny care for him. Unfortunately she died of a heart attack while caring for him. (Grand-dad came to live with our family after her death.)

When I heard the news of her death, I was devastated. I still remember that horrible, intense pain which choked and engulfed me. I ran to my room and threw myself on the bed.

My mind was blank in pain, shock and disbelief. Time seemed to have stopped. Then, the strangest occurrence happened. I began to be filled with the familiar rosy, reddish, warm feeling of warmth and love. It was like my Granny's arms were around me, and I could smell the wonderful odor of her body.

She told me she was very happy, that the next life is peaceful and loving, and that I was to be happy that she was happy. Although I could not see her, I knew she was there, embracing me. I'll never forget how she infused my body and my Spirit with peace, light, love and joy.

A naysayer might say that this was just my imagination. I say this was the Spirit of my Granny, and I *know* she was there.

CHAPTER 2

Children's Spirits See Truth

The world of reality has its limits; the world of imagination is boundless. - Jean Jacques Rousseau

The events in this chapter happened in late 1939 and concern our lives as children, our friends and activities.

Our house was across a gravel road from a tiny forest at the Lake Shore Gold Mine's property in Kirkland Lake, Ontario. The mine's landscaper had allowed the trees to remain since they hid the place where they stored their old mining equipment.

In between the little forest and the mine had been a lake, which, sadly, the mine had filled with mine tailings. (In those days there didn't seem to be any government requirements regarding maintaining our natural resources. We kids called that area "the slimes," which seemed like a good name for it.)

During the winter, we skated on one of the water holes that had not yet closed over in the slimes, and in summer we sometimes played on all the old wires and mining equipment which had been dumped there. We all knew we weren't supposed to go there, but sometimes, when we were bored, we played there anyway.

The mine employed a man to look after all the old, rusting equipment and we children named him the "dump man." One of his jobs was to keep people away from the equipment, which was often sold to other mining companies. The "dump man" would chase us off the slimes often - if he caught us.

The equipment was absolutely marvelous to play on. There were long ladders made of heavy, rusty iron that had been used underground, connecting one level to the next as an escape hatch in case of emergency.

As children tend to do, we used our imaginations freely. We played cowboys and robbers; we held up imaginary trains and, despite warnings from our parents, we didn't give a hoot about all that rust. We hung upside down on the tall iron ladders. When the "dump man" was around, we hid in or behind what looked like vats and upside-down containers. Sometimes we would hide in the small containers on wheels that looked like small train cars.

My mother always made me go out to play with my brother, Terry. Generally Terry and I got along well, and I sure looked up to my big brother. However, having me tag along with his gang- the "Lake Shore Gang" as it was called, was quite another situation and he wasn't at all pleased about it initially. Terry was the leader of this little group of about six boys ages anywhere from 6 to 8 years old. After being accepted into the gang, the other boys seemed to enjoy my company - even though I was a "guurrrl." I was the smallest member of Terry's gang but I managed to keep up with the boys' games and hikes and anything else they conjured up. Terry was my hero as a child and all through our lives in adulthood, and still is, even though he has crossed the veil into a new dimension.

Summertime was such a fun time. Even when it rained, we had things to do, like designing costumes from mom's old clothes or making masks, and then putting on plays in the garage. We charged the neighborhood girls a couple of pennies to come and see our play.

Most of the time - at least for the plays - my older sisters, Margaret and Pat, would help by giving suggestions and applying the finishing touches, as well as manning the curtains, being the announcers and collecting the entrance fees.

I was the youngest in my family and also in the gang. The smallest kid in the town's other organized youth group - the "Main

Street Gang" - was a little fellow named Dickey Duff. If the Lake Shore Gang and the Main Street Gang got bored, we would meet each other by going through the hole in the fence which separated our property from the town. And then we would fist fight, just for something to do.

I used to beat up Dickey until I thought he wanted to cry, but he held it back. I knew I could "take him" anytime. Then Dickey Duff grew . . . and I didn't.

Dick Duff grew up to be a professional hockey player for the Toronto Maple Leafs and played for other national hockey teams, but back in 1939 or 1940 he was just Dickey Duff, my opponent in "fistycuffs."

When September came, the older children went to school and I was left alone. There was no kindergarten in our area at that time, so I was left to my own resources. The Lake Shore Mines had made a lovely little playground with sand and swings and a teeter-totter, as well as a maypole-like swing. This was situated on the edge of the little forest. Although mom had instructed me *not* to enter the forest unless I was with one of my sisters or brother, I still went in alone, being lured there by the call of birds or a scampering chipmunk. I loved the forest, the trees, wild flowers, the little birds and animals, and I spent a great deal of time discovering the wonders of nature. It was there that I also discovered new dimensions both in language and Spirit.

Pierre and Marie

There are voices which we hear in solitude, but they grow faint and inaudible as we enter into the world - Ralph Waldo Emerson.

It was on one of my forest outings that I first met Pierre and Marie. They were French and brother and sister. They appeared behind me unexpectedly one morning. I never even heard them come.

Pierre and Marie spoke only French and they began teaching me, starting with touching face, ears, mouth and saying the French words. I was enchanted with the sound of their voices, their laughter and that melodic new language. I began picking up the lovely new words. We played in the forest, but they would not come onto the "slimes" with me. I remember wanting to show them how, if a person jumped up and down in the same place on the slimes long enough, the water would ooze up above the slime and make a really big puddle.

Marie, Pierre and I had fun together and I enjoyed being with them. One thing I noticed was that they never fought. They both had lovely, curly dark hair; Pierre's was short, and Marie's longer. Both of them had brown eyes like mine. They were a few years older than me and I often wondered why they were not in school.

Even though we could not talk together much, I still learned more and more French words. Another thing I noticed was that they were always there when I came and I guessed they didn't go home until after I left. I never met their parents, nor did I ever hear anyone call them for lunch, or come and get them to go to their home.

My mom was unaware of my new playmates until she realized I was beginning to use French words in my vocabulary. She was curious about where I was learning French. Mom was a very busy lady, with four young children and many other interests, and she must have let the matter drop. However, mom had been a teacher and I heard her wondering aloud as to why Marie and Pierre weren't in school. I also overheard her telling dad about my new playmates and asking him if there were any French employees in the mine.

"Of course there are many French-speaking miners," he said, and they both dropped the subject. It was a while later, just before the snow, and I wondered why Pierre and Marie didn't wear warmer clothes. I mentioned this to mom. I remember she looked puzzled, and then sent my oldest sister, Margaret, to go with me and meet Pierre and Marie. It was Saturday morning in October and I didn't think they would be there on a weekend. They weren't there then and I never saw my young French friends again.

Pierre and Marie had given me a real love of French people and also the language. Although I had difficulty learning French in school, I picked it up quickly when I lived in Quebec. Is it possible that Spirit paves the way for many experiences which occur in our lives? I often wonder about Pierre and Marie who so often appeared to me out of nowhere. Were they children who had died long ago but still came to play? Were they sent there to protect me from my own inquisitive nature? Who knows? All I know is that it was wonderful while it lasted.

I remember my mother telling me that Marie and Pierre were not real, but simply part of my imagination. Even at that age, I knew what I saw was a reality and I believed in it. I am so thankful that I did not allow anyone to obliterate this intuitive gift from the Spirit world. Maybe mom was partially right in the fact that because I was open to life, the imagination allowed me to see what others couldn't.

I think we all have the capability of looking into other dimensions and of thinking with Spirit. We need to take the time and space. We need to stop filling ourselves up with noise. We need to appreciate the "gift of silence" where we can talk and listen to our Spirits.

Francine, one of the members of our writers' group said to me: "DorisMae, perhaps you might think about mentioning this experience to other people. They may think you're crazy."

First of all, I don't really care what other people are thinking, but I do have a question. How does a five-year-old child who plays alone in the forest start learning French words? When Marie and Pierre came it seemed a real blessing to me. They kept my interest so I did not go onto the "slimes." They were miracles for me and kept me safe.

Noise comes with speed, where everything we do is sped up. People seem to have a need to turn on their radios, cell phones, iPods, text machines or TVs and have forgotten the blessings and the quiet of silence, where Spirit lives.

CHAPTER 3

Thank Heavens for our Universal God!

Your desire is in your prayers. Picture the fulfillment of your desire now, and feel its reality, and you will experience the joy of your answered prayer - Dr. Joseph Murphy

In the Tucson (Arizona) Daily Star I read an ad headed: "NO GOD; NOW WHAT?"

Apparently the writer's aim was to support the idea there is no God and why reason, experience and science - as opposed to faith, revelation and trust - should be the foundations and guideposts for humanity's progress.

When my husband, Ray, and I had breakfast at the OverPass Café, in Tucson, I spotted a man with a white beard wearing a T-shirt which had the inscription: "God is Good!" I complimented him on his choice of T-shirt, and we struck up a conversation.

During the talk, I mentioned the newspaper ad and the man, whose name was Donny Rohrback, summed up his feelings with a wonderful one liner: "If there is no God, why advertise it?"

Without a God, life must be such an empty bore.

I am so thankful for our Universal God. Many times I have written to God, and I've received some wonderful answers. Fortunately, I've kept them safe in my journals. Try it sometime if you haven't already. The experience, I'm certain, will be rewarding. I don't know how I would live without God. He/She has been with me always.

This is an excerpt from my journal dated Oct. 7, 2002:

Father, I want you to bless two people from my past, and I want to tell you their stories. My husband, Ray, and I were talking about Valentine's Day, and as I related this memory to him we were both deeply touched, realizing fully both the depth of tragedy and pathos in the past circumstances. At the time I lived in this story, I was very young, and had no idea of the terrible tragedy unfolding.

Go ahead.

The first episode concerns a Valentine 's Day in Grade 4; when this took place Barry was a small boy in my class who always looked dirty, and smelled bad; like he slept in his clothes and perhaps wet the bed in his clothes at night. His little pointed chin, his small brown eyes and tough expression belied the streaks of tears I often saw on his high cheek bones. The whole class had made valentines and that morning we gave them out to the people we had made them for. I had made lots of valentines and gave one to everyone in the class.

In return, I received a bundle of them. Barry only got one. That was the one from me. We all went home at noon time and when I returned to school after lunch Barry was waiting for me.

He had a big white envelope in his hand and insisted it was for me, but I was not to open it until I got home. Since we had a Valentine's Day party in class, with white icing and red candy hearts decorating all the way around the cake, I must have shoved the envelope in my book and forgot about it. Barry waited for me after school and implored me not to open it until I got home. He even walked me all the way home, too.

When I got into my house I told my mom about the incident

and we both opened the big white envelope together. Inside was a beautiful "store bought" Valentine's Day card, with big purple and burgundy pansies inside a red valentine on the front of the card, and a nice poem about caring for each other inside. There was also a neatly folded cotton hanky, bordered in white, with blue, purple, and burgundy colored pansies in the middle part.

My mom stared at the hanky and card a long time and then murmured: "I wonder where he got this card. I wonder where he had the money to buy the hanky." She patted me on the shoulder and left me to wonder, too.

Barry was the second oldest child of seven children. His dad was tall and brown skinned. He drank a lot and I often saw him swaying back and forth as he walked back from the beer parlor. He beat Barry and the younger boys a lot, too. Barry often came to school with a dirty face smeared with tear marks which he had wiped off with his tattered sleeve.

My mom sometimes quietly took food to his mom, when Barry told me she was so sick she couldn't get up. They lived in a house on the other side of the fence and there was a big hole in the fence right outside their place. That's where we went through to take a shortcut to school.

Barry's older sister, Clara, failed a grade and landed in my class in Grade 8. Then she dropped out of school and I saw her sitting outside her house one day looking very unhappy. She had a big tummy and when I asked Barry about her, he said she was going to have a baby; that her father had thrown a party with some of his friends and they had all taken Clara to bed that night.

So God, I know it's very late to bless Barry and Clara, and to help them, and I don't know what happened to either one of them, or to their brothers. Someone said Barry was in jail, but I never really knew if that was true and to be honest, Father, I was too busy in my own life to give them much thought at that time. The pure, stark tragedy of their lives unfolded within me today when I told my husband, Ray, about them, and I sit now, telling you, and I'm crying again.

So please bless them and give them your warmth and your love and know that I do care for them, and feel so bad that they had such a miserable time growing up when we went to school together. Please tell Barry I kept the hanky a long time and often wondered about that Valentine's Day. I know I told him "thanks for the card and hanky" because his face smiled. I had never seen him smile till then. So please tell him "thanks again for the card and hanky" and thanks, Father, for taking care of them.

DorisMae, thank you for caring; I have taken care of both of them. One is just fine now and I'm watching over the other and the brothers.

Thanks Father. I sure love you.

Continuing on with our universal God

There was a time when I belonged to a church which considered itself "the only true church "on earth. It was difficult to extricate myself from this church for I was assured that I would go to hell.

In desperation I prayed for the answer and it came in the form of another "bright dream."

The dream started with me beginning to fly, high in the sky, with a guide which I did not see at first, since he was flying above me. He told me to look below.

The sky beneath us was filled with many airplanes. My guide pointed and said: "The planes represent the various churches. The one right below us, which looks like a metal pterodactyl with all the rivets and joints in the wings, is the church you just left recently."

My guide then flew a little ahead of me and I could see him pointing to other planes and identifying them. "Over there is the Anglican church, and farther over is the Presbyterian. Right over there is the plane representing the Muslim faith. And see that small bright colored plane, that's the atheist one. He went on and on, identifying the many different planes. Then he asked: "Do you notice something very important? They are all flying in the same direction. They are all flying home."

That dream was a very powerful statement as to who is in charge of us all. He/She is our universal God.

CHAPTER 4

The Spirit of our Earth's Birds and Animals

Our worlds of birds, trees, plants, animals, rocks and all of Nature; these have their own special Spirit and are here to teach us - DorisMae Honer

There was a report in the Denver Co. newspaper how a parrot saved a little girl's life by screeching "mama, baby" over and over until the babysitter saved the choking little girl by using the Heimlich maneuver. I wonder why some members of our humankind find it so hard to believe that we are not the only beings who can sense danger, or can figure out a problem, or can think and feel.

There have been reports of dogs alerting emergency services that their master was in trouble, and the medical people who came to attend to the ailing person saved the person because of the dog's intervention.

My dad witnessed an old squirrel putting nuts carefully onto a narrow golf course road. He noticed that the squirrel had no teeth. The squirrel waited patiently for a car to pass and then went to retrieve the inner nuts from the broken shells on the road. The squirrel had figured out how to use cars to open the nuts he had gathered.

I am so happy that our God in all His/Her wisdom has made all living things able to sense, feel and think, because more and more, as world events evolve , it is apparent that everything has a soul. In his book "The Power of Myth," Joseph Campbell mentions often the importance of having a connection with the natural world. He says, "if you will think of ourselves as coming out of the earth, rather than having been thrown here from somewhere else, you see that we are the earth, we are the consciousness of the earth. These are the eyes of the earth. And this is the voice of the earth."

National Geographic has many TV specials on the different habits and feelings which are shown by the animals of the forest and jungle. For example, mother love is a universal feeling enjoyed by all living creatures. The care that animals give to their newborns is extraordinary. They have a gift for feeling, what others are going through, and helping in their own ways, like the parrot that saved the choking little girl by screeching "mama, baby" to the babysitter.

Let me tell you about a parrot named Connie. My friend, Denise lived around the corner from me for years. She received this little green bird as a gift from her husband, Steve. But first I'll fill you in on the details which lead up to Connie.

Denise had been taking care of her mother, Renee, who was lively and adorable in her own unique way. Renee was a keenly astute business woman who had built a very fine reputation in the wholesale bicycle business. She worked with her husband and sold bicycles worldwide. Her wonderful sense of humor endeared her to all who knew her, and her tiny well dressed appearance was always a joy to behold. Renee sometimes complained that her marriage was difficult and, eventually, she left her husband when she was 80 and set up her own home close by Denise.

As time went by, Renee's health failed and she needed occasional care; then, little by little, constant care. Denise was up to the task and took care of her mom daily, attending to her every need.

She is a person who has "given of herself" all her life. When her mom was dying, she cared for her every moment. Eventually, Renee died in her daughter's arms. Denise's favorite saying is one she quotes from Judy Garland: "Never settle for being a second-rate copy of someone else. Be a first-rate edition of *yourself*."

Connie was a gift to Denise after her mother died. Connie

seemed to understand the grief which Denise was feeling. Connie became a healing spirit who helped Denise find her own balance again, and made her laugh, just like her mom had done for so many years.

Denise has the natural spirit which animals and birds are drawn to and trust. She has birds coming to her for care, like the newborn sparrow someone had placed on her doorstep. That sparrow is so close to Denise and such a character! Denise introduced me to her birds and animals and described their different personalities in depth. Perhaps I should mention something else which Denise has in common with her natural menageries. For example, have you ever seen an animal who has lost a leg keep on living a natural life, despite the affliction? Wonderful, isn't it? Before I go on too much further, I have to mention that Denise suffered terrible damage when she was in her twenties. She was hit by a car. She regained most of her abilities, but has a few serious residual problems because of the accident. Does that stop her? Not on your life. When I visit Denise, I go into a different world and feel the peaceful Spirit as well as the whimsy, found mostly in nature.

Denise has an artistic nature and her drawings and paintings of nature's birds, animals and fish are beautiful. Her canvases are rocks, as well as the usual canvases most artists paint on and she paints with real tranquility and a deep feeling of serenity. She makes me feel happy when I'm with her.

I remember Denise for many reasons and the one which first drew me to her was her great love and understanding of animals which is totally reciprocated by any animal or bird who is in her vicinity. Someone brought a baby woodpecker to her one morning. Denise cared for the little bird, with the idea of letting it go when it was fully grown. That day came and Denise brought "Woody" to the door, talked to him gently and opened the door, encouraging him to fly away. Woody took to the air and was gone. Later in the afternoon Denise went out again and there was Woody sitting on the fence waiting for her. He flew right back into the house and onto his cage.

She tried for several days, but noticed the wild birds ganging up on him. So Woody stays in except for his morning flights. Denise is "at one" with all the Spirits of birds and animals.

Denise and I keep contact through the email. She sent me photos of her latest artistic work and she has blossomed. Her art critics have been very positive in their encouragement. Denise keeps in touch with artists via the Internet. A fellow artist, Kristin Hubick, (from Retro Café Art, Indianapolis, Indiana) says, "Denise Phillip's mixed media work embodies the beauty of nature with a touch of whimsy. She uses various elements to tell a story or recreate a memory, leaving the viewer wanting more."

If you don't believe that dogs, cats, birds, mammals have Spirit; just ask anyone who works in an SPCA, or any veterinarian who cares deeply for his/her work. I am sure that in your own lives you have met many people like Denise who care for God's many creatures with such love in their hearts. I'm sure you have witnessed the love and trust God's creatures give back in return. There must be a million or more stories of the faithfulness and love that pets have given to their masters.

As I write about the Spirit found in animals, and some people, I want you all to read an article written by Shirley S. Barret, who is a member of our writer's group at Gordon United church in Victoria, British Columbia. Shirley is writing her memoires with the intention of including them all in a book for her family. Shirley was originally from the United States, and has come to live in Canada near one of her children. She is an intelligent and classy lady with a real appreciation for humor, as well as a deep sensitivity to Spirit. Shirley is a wonderful writer. When Shirley writes, she touches our hearts with her deep insights and observations into life. We decided together to include one of her stories here, since the anecdote is a clear example of the fact that a beautiful Spirit dwells in all God's creatures.

Just Be There. ━━━━━━━━━━━━━━━━━━━━━━━━━

By Shirley S. Barrett

We had bought a home in Oregon in 1989, preparing for our retirement. We were now a family of four, since my mom had come to live with us. We all called her Mom. My husband Bob and I were retiring and although son Harry was working, he still wanted to live "at home". We were so excited as we moved into our new home. Our neighbors had come over to introduce themselves and we knew we were going to enjoy them. They were very helpful, giving us information about our new community, and simply were very amiable people.

I am a very early riser. Now that we were settled I was enjoying a hot cup of coffee on our patio, watching the dawn stretch across the sky. What a pleasure to listen to the quiet, enjoy the freshness of the early morning and not to have to hurry anywhere. Halfway through my first cup, I saw her. She was sitting on the fence, a nice smooth black, gray and white cat, and she was looking right at me. I spoke to her softly, encouraging her to come closer. After several minutes she jumped down and disappeared around our neighbor's house on their side of the fence. The same thing happened the next morning. On the fourth morning she jumped down on our side of the fence, settling herself on the lawn. About five mornings later she surprised me by coming onto the patio and jumping up into my lap. She looked up at me, purring softly. The more I talked to her, the more she purred. What a wonderful way to begin my day. She was our neighbor's cat and her name was Sandy.

In my family it was my sister who was the cat person, where as I was always the dog lover. Bob and I had plans to get a dog, and a few days later Bob, Mom and I went to the SPCA to look them over. Although my favorite dog is a collie, our yard was too small for a large dog. I saw a sheltie and was considering him when my husband Bob called me over. "Look at this one, cute isn't she?" he said smiling broadly. I couldn't believe my eyes. The dog was a long way from being cute. She was very skinny, about eight pounds with very ragged blond hair and a pushed short pointed snout, a medium long tail, and a strange mixture of other dog characteristics. While other dogs were barking, she was very quiet. Bob put his hand through the fence and over she came to happily lick his hand. I asked the SPCA lady if we could take her out. When Bob held her she cuddled up in his neck. When he handed her to Mom, she quickly cuddled up to Mom and kissed her cheek, which made Mom react saying, "She's so cute, Bob, she can sleep in my bed." This exclamation was from Mom who had once said firmly that, "all dogs should remain outside, since inside was for humans only!"

We took the dog. Her name was Snoopy.

Snoopy took us over the minute she was in the car. She sat on Mom's lap all the way home. However, she and I had a long way to go yet, after she chewed through the handle of the leather covering on our indoor Jacuzzi. Then I caught her chewing on the leg of our sofa. I scolded her and put her outside, suggesting to her that she chew on a tree. Oregon had lots of them. Bob bought two ropes at the Pet Store, both about a foot and a half long with a big knot in the center of them. Snoopy had taken to coming out with me on the patio in the early morning, when I enjoyed my hot cup of coffee. On the second morning we both saw Sandy sitting on the fence. Snoopy ran across the lawn jumping up against the fence. Sandy didn't move. I felt sorry for Sandy. We had just become friends, and I was going to miss our "purr" times together. I checked with Sandy's family and got permission to give her treats, so from then on, each of the following early mornings I took a snack to the fence and shared it between Snoopy and Sandy. The friendship grew between dog and cat in the early mornings, weather permitting. On Snoopy's fourth early morning with us she brought her rope out onto the patio thrashing it from side to side, but when she let go, the rope flew up into the air and fell splashing into my cup of coffee. Hot coffee splattered all over my robe. I sat very still, then looking straight into her eyes I said, "We have 10 days to try you out or replace you. You are awfully close to being replaced by the sheltie I liked."

On Snoopy's eleventh day we sent Snoopy to be groomed, and when she returned she looked so fluffy and cute. She was now part of the family. Snoopy became the most lovable, intelligent dog that we have ever owned. In the afternoon she belonged to Mom, snuggling beside her on Mom's bed at nap time. During night time she belonged to Bob. She was always at his side. Snoopy, Sandy and I continued to share our early mornings together. Sandy continued to tease Snoopy, always staying a safe distance away, but coming just enough safely close each morning. As time went on they spent a lot of time together by that fence.

It had been some time since 1989 when Snoopy had come to live with us. Mom had passed away in 1994, and the year was now 2002. Bob had died last August.

One day I looked out the patio door and saw a strange sight. Something was wrong. Sandy was lying on the edge of our grass and Snoopy was sitting quietly beside her, looking towards our house. Slowly I went outside. As I approached, Sandy didn't move. Snoopy moved over a few inches, and had a worried look on her face. I hadn't seen Sandy for about three days and she looked like she had lost a lot of weight. I went to the garage, picked up Snoopy's bath towel, went back and wrapped Sandy gently in it and brought her into the house. Snoopy followed closely behind and we all sat on the couch together. I talked to Sandy softly. She opened her eyes attempted a purr, looked at Snoopy and then closed her eyes and seemed to go back to sleep again.

No one was home at Sandy's house. Some of the family had gone to the coast to fish, and wouldn't be home until tomorrow. However, their oldest girl, who was in college, would be home around 4:30. I wasn't sure if the oldest son was still in town. About an hour later I heard a car in their driveway, so I lay Sandy down on her side, with her back supported by the sofa's back. Snoopy crawled in beside her protecting her from falling off the sofa's edge, and providing warmth to her. I made another call, and in a few minutes Brian, their son, came to get Sandy. He explained that they were concerned about Sandy and had taken her to the vet. The vet had found nothing wrong that he could fix. He had explained that Sandy's 20 year old body was beginning to wear out, and she would be gone soon. I wondered how Sandy had been able to jump up and over the fence, in her condition. I remembered that Snoopy hadn't even barked at her. When Brian and Sandy left, Snoopy jumped back up on the sofa where Sandy had lain.

Two mornings after I had found Sandy in the grass beside our fence, I took Snoopy for a walk. On our return, we were headed for the front door. There on the sidewalk close to our front step was Sandy lying just below the step. I thought she was dead. There were flies on her eyes and she gave no movement. I put Snoopy inside the house, got a towel and wrapped Sandy in it, brushing the flies away from her eyes. Then I carried Sandy, with Snoopy following close behind out onto the patio. The day was beautiful and bright. Holding Sandy in my arms, I sat down on one of the chairs close to the table; Snoopy jumped up to sit on the other chair beside me. She wiggled around until she placed her head on my knee, close to Sandy's head. We three sat there a long time, quietly together. Our son Harry had been working and I expected him home about 6:00 in the evening. I heard a car come into the neighbor's driveway. When our neighbor's son Brian came to his back door, I called him over, and he took Sandy home. The next morning Brian's dad Dave, phoned and told me they had taken Sandy to the vet and had her put to sleep. Snoopy seemed to know. She lay around for several days, and when out, she would run to the fence, and sniff around. She finally understood that Sandy would not come back. I think she grieved awhile.

I am going to miss Sandy too. The fence will never look the same. Can an animal like Sandy look for comfort in her time of need? Whatever Sandy's reason for crawling with great effort to our house, she put new thoughts into my mind. Did Snoopy really understand Sandy's needs in those last days? I believe she did. Snoopy just sat quietly with Sandy, at her side. She never barked or made a fuss. Snoopy didn't need words or answers. Snoopy knew she needed to "just be there" with her friend Sandy to comfort her in her time of need.

CHAPTER **5**

Omens-What significance are Omens?

To know what you prefer instead of humbly saying "Amen" to what
the world tells you that you ought to prefer, is to have kept your soul
alive - Robert Louis Stevenson

In Paulo Coelho's book, The Alchemist, the king speaks to a
shepherd boy about omens. Omens are unusual occurrences or the
appearance of certain things - alive or otherwise - which warn of
things to come.

What do dreams mean to all of us? There are many people
interested in the meaning of dreams, psychologists and psychiatrists
included. There must be some interesting significance in dreams. I
like to examine dreams, and know the difference between dreams
and visions. The visions which come when asleep are like dreams,
but brighter, and slower in action. Dreams are often considered
omens, and bring their own power to help.

There is another immense power, the one found in the greatest
kingdom on earth, the kingdom of nature, birds, animals, rocks,
insects, fish, plants and trees. Many of us, especially in the city,
are oblivious as to the impact this natural kingdom has upon us.
Oblivious that is, until a major earthquake happens and impacts us
in some way, whether it is direct involvement or in compassion for
those hit and affected.

My astrology sign is Libra, represented with the balancing scales, and Libra's element is the air. Perhaps this is why the appearance of birds in odd circumstances may be omens for me.

An example: When I was only three, workmen had left a ladder propped against the sloping roof above our porch after having removed storm windows on my parents' bedroom windows. For some reason they left early, forgetting to take down the ladder. What a temptation!

You can imagine the wonderings of a three year old child as to what it would be like to sit on the roof! That little DorisMae climbed the ladder onto the sloping roof. She was curious and unafraid of the height. She sat on the rough, sloping roof shingles and quietly looked down upon the little forest across the street from our home.

A robin came and perched on the roof beside her. She knew that if she kept real still, the robin would not fly away. So the robin sang and she kept very still, listening intently. She was so intent on watching and listening to the robin, that her mind took a mental snapshot.

I still can see that robin on the sloping shingles in my mind's eye, singing its little heart out. (I believe to this day that my Spirit guides sent the robin to distract me and keep me still.) My parents came walking down the street toward home. Mr. Robson, a friend, was with them. When they spotted me on the roof, mom fell over in a faint and Mr. Robson caught her.

My dad, meanwhile, came running across the lawn and climbed up the ladder like a monkey. The robin flew away and dad brought me – protesting all the way - carefully down the ladder.

Was it coincidence? I don't think so. I believe our world of nature is a very important part of our existence and if we are connected to it, we enjoy a greatly enriched life. I also think that the unseen community of our Divine Spirits sends these little creatures along to help us.

Later, when I was five or six, I used to play with a little boy next door. His name was Tommy Ramsay. He was an only child, and I was the youngest of four children in a very busy family. I liked to play with Tommy and tell him I was his big sister. We had a very special relationship. When Tommy was three or four he was caught in between a car and a trailer and died. After his funeral, we kids were outside on the porch of the Ramsay house. It was spring.

Suddenly, five bright yellow canaries flew onto the porch railing. They perched there and sang, warbling and twittering for the longest time, seemingly unafraid of our presence.

Astounded, we marveled at the canaries and their beautiful songs long after the little yellow birds had flown away. My dad said he didn't think canaries came this far north so early. What a feeling of wonder! The actions and songs of these little canaries impacted us for our lifetime.

Was this, too, just another coincidence? Not on your life. Tommy loved canaries.

In 1987, I was on my own and had rented an apartment in Gravenhurst, Ontario. I was at my kitchen window doing dishes when I saw something in the trees move slightly. It was perched about 10 feet from my window. I stood motionless, watching, and then in wonder recognized the magnificent Golden Eagle. Silently, the bird spread its enormous wings and flew with quiet grace through the trees and disappeared. I wondered what the eagle had come to tell me. (I later found out that the large bird was a herald to me of imminent change coming into my life)

Shortly after seeing the Golden Eagle, my work conditions took a very unfortunate turn and it became imperative that I move. I moved south, closer to my son, Robert, in southern Ontario. My life stabilized there and then I moved once more, this time far north, to care for my mother who had suffered a stroke. It was there, while working in a chronic-care residence, that I met Bryan. He had come to visit his mother there. Bryan and I enjoyed almost 10 years together.

Although he had serious medical problems, we found great happiness together. However, as the years progressed, Bryan suffered increasingly with the many chronic illnesses which, despite all efforts, were becoming worse with time. His doctors asked me to come in one afternoon. They told me that Bryan had very little time to live; maybe six weeks, maybe six months. There wasn't any hope. He had too many strikes against him.

This was shocking and painful news. I had to work that evening and later, when I was driving home, I was still numbly trying to think on what to do. Great white snowflakes had fallen on the snow banks, yet the sky was now clear and the moon bright and full, charging the diamond-studded snow in sparkling rainbow colors of pinks, purples, yellows and blues. The surrounding white landscape flashed and glittered in the forest on Good Fish Lake where we lived and the night was filled with the quiet beauty only nature can provide.

As I drove that wintery country road closer to home I wondered to myself: "How can I help Bryan?"

It was then that magic happened. A huge snowy owl flew directly over the hood of my car, wings outspread, soft and white, with spots of black here and there. What a wonder! For me, time stood still. I was entranced with the grace and beauty of that huge bird.

Was that bird sent to give me courage, a message? Was this bird also an omen of change? I wondered.

It was on that starry, moonlit night that I made my decision. Shortly after "the night of the snowy owl," I packed Bryan into the car and we headed south. When we got to Tucson, Arizona, we stayed in a Holiday Inn. I watched Bryan perk up and begin to walk with more confidence. Inside myself, I heard a voice say to me: "This is the place."

We found a nice, comfortable place to live, in a 55-and-over park, and he started a business in Tucson. Meanwhile I took Reiki lessons from a lady in the church where we went, and gave Bryan Reiki sessions off and on when he asked for them. Reiki is a hands on healing energy which helped him relax. Bryan lived four more wonderful years, which, incidentally, were full of fun and frolic. We also travelled.

His last four years were worthwhile and valuable for both of us, as well as the environment business he had started. Before he died, Bryan gave me a puppy, a miniature poodle called Charlie. This little fellow was my close and very dear friend.

Once, when Charlie was little, I had let him out to relieve himself and was distracted for a moment. To my horror a roadrunner flew up to him. I ran out and picked Charlie up and brought him into the house. That roadrunner flew up onto the lamp outside our door and peered into our window, focusing on Charlie. Roadrunners eat little animals and will even fell a big animal like a cow, by pecking out their eyes.

I enjoyed Charlie as part of our family for more than nine years. Unfortunately, he was having trouble with his teeth. The day I took him to have his teeth extracted, I saw a roadrunner across the street. I wondered to my inner self: Is this an omen? It was.

Charlie later died in a tragic accident and our hearts were deeply saddened over losing him.

Paulo Coelho writes in his book, The Alchemist, of when the old woman speaks to the shepherd boy, she says: "In order to find the treasure, you will have to follow the omens. God has prepared a path for everyone to follow. You just have to follow the omens that He left for you."

Trust - that's what we seem to need - to recognize the omens, to believe in them and to follow their directions. That takes a lot of faith, as well as powers of observation.

As I mentioned before, my own astrology sign is Libra and its element is the air. I believe that this is why birds seem to be the messengers of change in my life. The more I write and think about omens, the more I realize that our native North American people knew what they were talking about, when they had a belief and trust in the powers of nature, and in omens.

Do you know what is your "reason for being" here on earth? Have you begun to follow your personal star? And besides your belief in God, have you connected with trust into the world of nature and omens? Have you begun to listen to the whisperings of the Spirit deep inside you? Do you record your dreams?

As French physiologist Claude Bernard once said: "Man can learn nothing except by going from the known to the unknown."

CHAPTER **6**

The Seed Bell and the Spirit of a Little Red Squirrel

Valiant spirits belong to all of life; to birds, animals, and nature as well as to humankind - Doris Mae Honer

My husband, Ray, and I bought the seed bell at a local market and Ray strung it up on a long wire suspended from a tall tree behind our home. We waited.

At first, no visitors came. Then one morning a little grey finch came by, perched on the seed bell and busily began pecking. Soon another and then another joined. It made perfect sense. The seed bell was designed for little finches. We were enthralled.

However, trouble sometimes comes on the heels of peace.

Our little grey finch family's new feasting ground was soon discovered. With raucous squawking and flapping of navy blue wings, with sharp beady eyes in black tufted heads, the Stellar's jays moved in. Although the tiny grey finches could easily hang onto the seed bell and peck away, the Steller's jays could not. They were too big.

Instead, they flapped around the bell, grasping it, and then fell away, except for the smaller female jays, which were able to hold onto the bell and peck at it for a short while. For several days the males kept up an awful riot, made dives and swoops at the bell until it eventually fell off onto a log below. Then the mob of jays attacked the seed bell with a loud, clamorous vengeance. The noise must have attracted the attention of a very tiny and curious red squirrel.

Soundlessly that little red squirrel dispatched the Steller's jays back into the trees, where they watched in noisy disbelief as the little newcomer began to devour what they considered their banquet. The little red squirrel also began a war with my husband Ray.

Ray shooed the little red squirrel away, picked up the seed bell remains and put them up on the picnic table. He then resumed watering the lawn. Quick as a wink the little red squirrel was on top of the picnic table munching away on her reclaimed prize. The bell was then marched firmly into Ray's house. The squirrel hopped onto the awning to peer into Ray's window and to keep track of *her* seed bell.

Inside the house, Ray, using that good, old household repair tool called masking tape, reattached the seed bell's wire. He then went to replace it on the cedar tree branch. Little red squirrel surveyed this new situation from her nearby tree.

Ray watched the following events with awe. Little red squirrel showed her true warrior spirit. From her perch in the tall cedar tree, she took a run, and a gigantic leap, and flew towards the bell, but missed. She rolled a bit right at Ray's feet; then up the tree she scooted again.

This time she took a sharper look at her course and decided a tree branch marred her vision. She therefore chewed off the offending branch and took aim again - a fast run; a huge leap and . . . CONTACT! Her little body clung victoriously to the swinging seed bell. After a few bites and much chattering to the audience of Steller's jays, the masking tape suddenly gave way and both little red squirrel and ragged seed bell came crashing to the ground, at the very feet of the astounded onlooker, my husband Ray.

Quick to assess this new threat, little red squirrel clasped the seed bell in her mouth. Alas, it was almost bigger than she was, and Ray was much bigger than she, so she dropped her bounty and scampered up the tree, chattering noisily at Ray. She sounded completely indignant about the whole situation. The seed bell came indoors for the night.

The next morning Ray went to work. The Steller's jays squawked and the little red squirrel chattered incessantly. I took the seed bell remains out, and laid them quietly on a log under her cedar tree. Then I left, leaving the little red victor to claim her spoils.

Our little red squirrel taught me again that inside each animal lays a very special Spirit, with feelings of courage and determination. They are all a gift to the earth and to humankind.

I'm hoping my readers agree and are kind to their pets and the animals in nature.

CHAPTER 7

Michael

We have forgotten the age-old fact that God speaks chiefly through dreams and visions - Carl Jung

The Labor Day weekend of September 1955 heralded the end of summer. It was about 7 p.m. when Michael arrived at the emergency department of the Royal Victoria Hospital in Montreal, Quebec.

Michael was 12, but small for his age, and looked a couple of years younger. He had sandy hair, a slightly freckled, sensitive face and clear green eyes. For his birthday, Michael had been given a bicycle he had wanted so dearly. He had been out riding around, getting used to the feel of his bike, when it happened.

Either he was uncertainly peddling his bike, or the speeding car simply did not see him, but the car smashed squarely into Michael, sending him high into the air. He came down onto the concrete sidewalk almost completely head first, spattering the concrete red, with blood, skin and tissue.

(The Royal Victoria Hospital stands at the corner of University Avenue and Pine Avenue West in Montreal, Quebec. It was established in 1893 by two Scottish immigrants and was not only a major health-care center, but also a focal point for learning.

In 1955, I was a student nurse in my last year of training, with six months to go. We called our hospital the RVH or the Vic, and were proud of her. We knew she was the foremost center of health care and learning in Canada at that time. The Royal Victoria Hospital was affiliated with McGill University, and all the students of medicine came there for part of their training.

At that time, the Vic's public wards comprised 15 beds lining each side, with a long wide aisle down the middle.

In the long ward, each patient was given privacy, when necessary, by drawing the curtains around the individuals' bed while treatments or private nursing care were given

At the head of the ward, situated on the other side of the nurse's station was the side room. It was generally used for the acutely ill. Patients there could receive more specialized care. There was ample room there for oxygen tents and tanks, suction equipment, intravenous solutions, intravenous blood as well as other equipment.

Ward D was a public surgical ward for men in one of the oldest wings of the Royal Victoria Hospital. At the time, afternoon and night shifts were staffed by the student nurse population, usually one senior, one junior, and a nurse's aide who generally had a fair amount of experience. There was also an orderly who assisted the male patients with bedpans and urinals and helped the nurses when asked.

During the afternoon and night shifts, the "charge nurse" was a senior student nurse who was generally in the latter part of her third year of training. She did treatments, dispensed medicines, assisted the intern doctors, and took vital signs of critically ill patients. She also wrote out doctors' orders in the patients' charts, sent prescriptions to the pharmacy or called the pharmacy for faster service when necessary.

The student was supervised by the evening supervisor who was a well- seasoned Registered Nurse (RN) who floated from ward to ward checking on everything. The senior nurse did all the charting on the very seriously ill patients. She also taught the junior student how to do dressings, treatments and charting as well as many other different aspects of nursing.

During the day, each ward had an RN in charge, and another as her assistant. The senior, junior and "probie" (probationary) student *nurses usually started their tour of duties on the day shift. When the senior and junior became accustomed to the ward routine, they were given evening and night shifts.)*

Michael was brought into the RVH emergency by ambulance and was accompanied by his uncle. In 1955, there were no big emergency units like there are in hospitals today.

There were a few rooms where the emergency staff did what needed to be done. If the patient needed further treatment, he or she was transferred to the operating room first and then sent to the appropriate ward.

Michael went straight to the operating room where they sent for specialists in neurology and orthopedics. X-rays were taken of his head and arm. Michael was also given blood and his broken arm was set. His head was bandaged after the doctors sutured the open wounds. He was given injections to protect him from infection.

Michael was not breathing well. Suspecting possible lacerations of his trachea, doctors performed a tracheotomy (the insertion of a device into the throat so he could breathe). They also inserted a gastric suction tube and another tube to drain and irrigate his bladder. When his vitals were stable, they tried to find a bed for him in a single room and a special nurse to take care of just him.

The hospital was packed with sick people and the "Vic's" children's ward was overcrowded as it was. There were no more available beds except the side room on ward D, men's surgical.

Since it was the end of summer, on the long Labor Day weekend, extra nursing staff was almost impossible to obtain, especially nurses with highly specialized neurology nursing skills.

Miss Cameron, our evening supervisor, could not find a special nurse from any of the agencies on that long Labor Day weekend.

I really liked Miss Cameron. She was a quiet, motherly, solidly built older nurse, proud of her Scottish heritage. Her light reddish hair was now almost completely white and she watched the world through intelligent, though faded blue eyes behind large glasses. She was known for her honest integrity as well as her shy gentle sense of humor.

Michael needed round-the-clock care. It was around 10:30 p.m. when he was brought to ward D, accompanied by the resident doctor, Miss Cameron and Michael's uncle, a nice looking and very worried young man of about 30. The doctor had given him permission to remain with Michael. I was the senior student nurse on duty that evening.

Miss Cameron knew I was in my last year of nurse's training, and had completed my six-month specialty stint in the Montreal Neurological Institute, or "the Neuro" as we called it then.

Miss Cameron said she was desperate, that she could not find a special night nurse anywhere because of the long weekend. I offered to do the night shift and she gratefully accepted. They had taught me well at the Neuro and I was well versed on "head injury" routine. Miss Cameron assigned me as Michael's special nurse.

In the Neuro we learned that anyone who is in a coma most probably can still hear, since the center for hearing is the last to remain in a person who is in a coma and near death. The hospital kept me on as Michael's special nurse for three more night shifts. His Uncle also took the night shifts, while Michael's parents were with him for days and evenings.

Suctioning the built-up mucous from Michael's tracheotomy was a very frequent job. The tube got blocked often.

His uncle and I turned him, rubbed him to increase his circulation and talked to him often, encouraging him to "hold on" and get better. I gave Michael my very best, treating him as if he was my very own son. We tried so hard to simply and gently "will him" to live.

Michael's uncle was a minister and our conversations were about life, and Spirit. He was an easy man to talk to and we both felt free to talk to God and to pray for Michael's soul as we cared for him.

At exactly 3:14 a.m. of the third night shift, I was turning Michael onto his other side after having rubbed his back when Michael opened his beautiful clear green eyes and looked straight into mine. My heart stood still. Then he took a shuddering breath. Michael died in my arms.

I still shed tears when I think of this, for looking into Michael's eyes for that short moment in time gave me a glimpse of Eternity.

Michael seemed to be telling me he was not afraid. He was just saying goodbye before his soul flew away. He taught me that death is sometimes a relief and a new beginning. He seemed to be telling me that there is nothing to fear.

I was distraught that we had not been able to save him. Two nights after he died, I had a very bright dream.

(My bright dreams are different from regular dreams. The bright dreams are gloriously bright in color and detail. The dream's rhythm is slower than regular dreams, giving me a chance to remember details.)

I was walking on a path up a rather oddly shaped mountain. Above me, I saw the figure of a young woman carrying a baby in her arms. She was walking down the path toward me, and I saw how beautiful she was, with long dark wavy hair and very large dark eyes. A long blue cape covered her shoulders and part of her long white gown. As she approached, she smiled at me. When she reached me, she quietly smiled again and with love, she placed her baby in my arms.

The enormity of her action struck me as I realized that she was Mary, the Mother of Jesus. Carefully and lovingly she placed her baby, the Christ child in my arms to hold.

I burst into tears as I held that beautiful son of God. I still weep when I tell this. It was a thank you from the Spirit World.

In 1958, on September 1 - Labor Day - I delivered my first baby, a boy.

Sylvia Browne states in her book Phenomenon: "Reincarnation is nothing more and nothing less than the belief that the human spirit, because it's eternal as a promise from God, survives the death of the body and returns to recurring lifetimes in a variety of chosen circumstances and bodies—i.e. incarnates again and again—for the purpose of growth and learning of the soul."

I have often wondered if my first son George might have been

Michael, or at least that they knew each other in the Spirit world.

I often think of Michael. I am so grateful to him for all that he taught me about Spirit. I believe that Spirit is common to all of us. All we have to do is open ourselves and listen.

CHAPTER **8**

A Spirit of Motherhood. (YES MOMMA, YOU'RE OUR STAR!)

Aim to be a woman of value, and success will follow - anonymous

Last night I watched the 2009 Oscar Awards on TV. How beautifully coiffed and gowned were the actresses. How slim they were, too, with deep cleavages showing plump breasts blatant in their sensuality. The men were handsome, clean shaven mostly, and all confident in their stardom. While I muted the many commercials, I had a chance to think back to the little girl I used to be. The grownups would ask me: "And what are you going to be when you grow up, DorisMae?"

My answer was always the same. With great confidence and an assured look, I would always reply: "I'm going to be a movie star!"

My memories shuttled back and forth to different stages in my own life. I outgrew the idea of becoming a movie star and replaced it with becoming a registered nurse. I then wanted a good husband and wished for six children. However, I had to settle for three. I think one of the special memories I love the most concerns my three much loved children.

At that time, Dr. Benjamin Spock had written a book, Baby and Child Care, and all we young mothers read it as religiously as a Bible.

When I was four months' pregnant, I told my oldest two that we were all going to have a baby. Being a nurse, I thought I'd better give them the news "straight" and none of this stuff about babies being delivered by a stork.

"Babies grow and come out from mommies' tummies," I explained in a matter-of-fact voice. Two pairs of large brown eyes bored holes at my little bump. "He can't be very big if he's in there," said Georgie, by then almost four.

Laura was quick to identify her sister: "She's going to be tiny like my doll. Oh mama, please order her to have long blonde hair, like Barbie's."(She must have been thinking of Sears catalogue). I was beginning to realize once again that these kids were way ahead of me.

As the time went along, two pairs of little hands explored my expanding stomach many times to see if the baby brother or sister would kick when they touched it. And their small mouths pressed against the tummy giving the new baby instructions on what it should be.

From Georgie: "I want you to run and jump like me, and to play horsey; and you can be the horsy."

Little Laura had her own thoughts: "I want you to play teacups with me and I won't let Georgie play - don't worry - because he always eats up all the cookies."

The baby's due date was around the middle of December and whenever I asked the two children about the baby I would get the same answer: "Baby is coming in December," followed by a firm nod of their heads.

They told everyone they knew that the baby was coming in December and would point to my tummy, saying: "He (or she, depending on the speaker) will get here before Santa Clause." I even heard my oldest telling the bread man: "I think Santa Claus will come early to our house."

I should have known better, but Dr. Spock said that well prepared and adjusted baby brothers and sisters are the ones who have been told the truths about the newborns coming into the family.

On Nov. 20, the contractions started. I called the babysitter in a panic. I heard my children tell her gravely: "Mommy's got a real bad stomach ache and has to go see the doctor. But she'll be OK, because the baby's coming in December."

I couldn't argue with them, or explain. They were too adamant and I was gasping too much for breath in between contractions.

In a few hours, baby Robert arrived. A few days later, I came home and Georgie looked at my somewhat deflated tummy and asked: "Where's the baby that was in there?"

I showed him Robert and he said: "Are you kidding? He was supposed to come with Santa Clause!"

Laura carefully tipped his little cap off his head and then, with hands on hips, she glared at me and shouted: "Where is her long blond hair?" before running away to her room and crying. Once she was reassured that baby Robert was indeed the baby who had been in mommy's tummy, she adjusted to the fact that he was a boy and became a wonderful sister to him.

The next morning, around 5 a.m., I was sitting in the living room nursing my newborn. I had been there awhile, thinking that I must comb my hair and stop looking like a tousled clown in my old ratty dressing gown and flannel pajamas. Then, two pairs of little feet came padding softly into the living room.

"What are you doing mom?" Laura and Georgie stood beside me peering into my open pajama top. "What's baby Robert doing in there?" they questioned.

Now was my time to explain about breastfeeding. I proceeded to tell them how I was giving the baby the best milk a mother could give from each of her breasts. Dr. Spock would have been proud.

For the first time I felt like a real STAR!

I think being a mother is the best stardom that God gives and for three little people I was a star.

George, Laura and Robert have grown up into adults who serve humankind with love and understanding. George works for the Utah Arts Council and reminds me of my grand-dad, who loved the native people and helped them to help themselves. George formed a Celtic band named Stone Circle and provides music entertainment for many people across the United States and Canada. George is so busy I cannot keep up with his progress. When he was growing up he kept his mouth zipped closed and I had to pry information out of him. He was extremely bright in school. He was an observer of all that went on around him, even when he appreared to be distracted or bored. He always came home with top marks and seemed to ace all his subjects. Music was his top priority. Our family went through a terrible tragedy when George's ex-wife and daughter Lena were involved in a terrible accident with an eighteen wheeler. Lena's mom was killed. Lena was paralyzed from the waist down. The story of George and Lena is still to be written, but enough to say that George and Lena worked hard together to get Lena rehabilitated. He was truly one of God's greatest sons in all his efforts and Lena is now living her life in a completely amazing way. George and I connect mostly by phone, and I tell him how much I love him. His dry sense of humor keeps us in stitches. He has married again and his wife Kristin is a beautiful, thoughtful and loving person. She let us know with great excitement that we are going to have another grandchild this September! (She delivered a baby girl who is as lovely looking, in miniature, as her mother.) I held baby Kyra, and was enchanted with the many expressions on her sweet little face.

Laura is a fine mediator in Victoria, B.C., Canada. Her clients speak highly of her compassionate service to them in their difficulties. She has also given workshops for companies to improve employee relations, worked with school boards and teachers as well as taking on personal clients. Laura is fun to be with, beautiful, compassionate and a very smart business woman. She was always smart with money, and as a little girl could buy Christmas presents for all of us on the small allowance she had saved up. Laura was a strong minded young lady growing up and had a hot Latin temper at times. I still remember her being very angry with me when I had to stop her from doing something, and she shook her little index finger at me and said, "Just wait. You just wait until I'm the mommy and you are my little girl." Laura has a good sense of humor, and we could always find common ground after our disagreements. Being the middle child, she learned mediation at an early age, and has used these gifts to benefit her profession.

Laura has given me five good looking grandchildren, two who have travelled worldwide, and the other three are learning to be contributing members of humankind as they journey into their chosen fields.

I love the deep, loving talks Laura and I have together. We seem joined together in Spirit, both of us understanding and able to observe more of the unseen Spiritual realm.

Robert works as clinical manager and therapist for a company which houses and cares for young people who have run amiss of the law. With his help, the group homes have expanded from one to six. Their programs involve schooling, athletics, arts and job counseling. He is also a consultant surveyor for the Commission for the Accreditation of Rehabilitation Facilities throughout Canada and the United States, helping their companies to meet all the qualifications required. When he was a little boy he was his sister's protector, and was never afraid of taking on any little boy who wanted to hurt his sister. I describe Robert's and my relationship simply-we grew up together. Even as a very young person he understood more deeply anything going on in his or my life. His sensitive insight into people and situations, as well as his sense of humor are acute, and well appreciated. He is very much loved. Robert has four children, all well loved and fascinating in their development, still too young to have chosen careers.

My children are the stars in my crown of motherhood. I love them so much. My eleven grandchildren are twinkling little stars in the milky way of new development. I am truly blessed.

CHAPTER 9

Experiences with the Universal Language of Spirit

Intuition is really a sudden immersion of the soul into the universal current of life, where the histories of all people are connected, and we are able to know everything because it is all written there
- Paul Coelho (The Alchemist)

In November of 1956, I married a Peruvian man, and in 1972 we went together to Mira Flores, Peru, outside of Lima, to visit his family.

While in Lima, we had attended a symphony concert and I was enchanted with the music of the featured harpist. I mentioned to the family that I wanted to learn to play the harp and would be interested in meeting the harpist. He also constructed Peruvian folkloric harps. The family contacted him, arranged that a harp be made and a meeting set up once the harp was completed.

The master harpist was a short, brown-skinned man with a barrel chest who grinned widely when he was pleased.

We had climbed up iron stairs to his apartment after first watching several children playing about the one faucet in the courtyard, spraying each other and then running away, laughing. Their mothers sat on the upper deck of the iron balcony, chatting with each other and watching the children.

The harpist spoke no English. He had constructed a harp for me and it was ready to be taken back to Canada. I knew nothing about playing a harp, but wanted to learn.

I spoke to him in Spanish and he shook his head. He spoke to me in Quechua, the native-American language of the people in the mountains of South America.

Although I didn't speak or understand Quechua, I knew he asked me if I wanted to play the harp. I answered that I did not know how. He began to show me, speaking in his native language.

I knew the language of music and listened intently. He showed me where C, G, D, and F were and began to play a simple Peruvian child's tune. By watching his strong fingers and listening to his quiet, melodious voice, I began to understand how to play the beautifully made Peruvian folkloric harp.

Somehow, we had communicated without understanding each others' verbal language. I believe we had spoken the universal language of the world. I believe it is the language of Spirit.

The harp was damaged slightly on the flight back to Canada. However, I loved it, and began to apply what I had learned from the master harpist. With three children and moving from place to place, I eventually had to give up my dreams of becoming an accomplished harpist. Therefore I phoned a harpist in Victoria, British Columbia, and offered my harp to her. She was delighted and I knew my harp would be used and appreciated.

Many years later, long after my first husband and I had parted in divorce, another story of the universal language of spirit occurred in Arizona. I had remarried to a very fine man named Bryan Morrison, and we were living in Tucson, Arizona.

Driving from Tucson, to Kirkland Lake, Ontario, Canada, I stopped in the north of Arizona by a roadside stand to buy some souvenirs for my grandchildren. My husband Bryan had preceded me for business reasons by plane. The salesman and I were haggling over prices when he asked how far I was going. I told him. He looked at me in a quizzical way and asked: "Are you alone?" I answered that I was, and then he questioned: "Aren't you afraid to be driving alone?" My answer seemed to astound him. I pointed at my car and said with a little tongue in cheek; "Really, I'm not alone. You just can't see who is in there. They are angels and there are so many they get their wings all tangled up. But sing? Oh, how they can sing!"

He looked at me in silence, and then packed up my gifts. Then he shook my hand, smiled, and said: "You'll have a very safe trip; that I know." He was a native American man, and I like to believe he understood the language of the Spirit. (My grandson, Kirk, said: "Grandma, he probably thought you were crazy!" Jared, another of my grandsons said, "Cool! He knew about Spirit.")

Along my route, I stopped at a rest station where I had lunch. Getting into my car, I didn't notice anything amiss, but as I was driving along, another car drove up beside me. There were two men in that car. One was pointing at my tires and gesturing that I had a problem and I should pull over.

I looked at them, and something – yes, the Spirit - told me they were dishonorable. I listened to my car and it was purring along beautifully. Flooring the accelerator I pulled quickly ahead of them and left them far behind. That night in the motel an announcer on TV news gave a warning to women driving alone. It involved two men who had pulled over a lady motorist after indicating she had car trouble. They had knocked her out and then took her to an isolated place, raped her, robbed her and stole her car. My angels had whispered their warnings and I had heeded their whispers.

I think dreams also speak the universal language. Bright dreams are also called "visions" and I learned this by reading my Bible.

Bryan had been ill for some time. Often, to help him relax, I gave him Reiki treatments. Reiki is the Japanese word for Universal life force energy. Briefly, it is a hands- on transference of energy which brings healing to the ill person through relaxation. I gave Bryan several treatments sometimes lasting almost an hour, and he said he felt better. He was able to sleep well after his treatments. Before he died I was visited by a shining being about four foot seven or eight - the size of my grandmother Honer, and the same size as Bryan's grandmother. She wandered about our bedroom and stopped beside Bryan for a moment and then disappeared. Bryan died several nights later. I believe she had come to tell me he would soon be leaving. About six or seven months after Bryan died, he came to me in a bright dream.

He brought with him a very beautiful woman and introduced her to me as his wife. He told me I was to marry and that there would be a very fine man coming into my life soon. Several months later someone I knew slightly became a close friend and later we fell in love. We were married awhile after Bryan went across the veil.

I have not forgotten Bryan and the wonderful, loving relationship we shared together, particularly when we moved to Tucson to start a life for just the two of us. Love doesn't die. I'm so glad he is in a loving relationship on the other side. Bryan came back to visit me once again, when I was working on a project at school. I know he was there because my dog Charlie started wagging his tail and looking into the doorway of our bedroom. Although I did not see Bryan, I felt his presence. He was pleased that I had started back to school, and interested in the project I was working on which was regarding the environment. Bryan had been an environmentalist assisting mines to meet the government regulations in mine openings and closures. I knew I was on the right track.

He is happy that Ray, my new and loving husband is taking good care of me.

CHAPTER **10**

Our Humankind's Spiritual Power

You must claim the events in your life to make yourself yours –
Anne Wilson Schaef, writer and psychotherapist

When attending a conference in 1993, I attended a workshop on psychology given by Dr. Charles Spezzano who said: "You are the star in your own life. You are your greatest in the worst of times, for the winds coming towards you allow you to soar."

Somewhere I copied down something else: "It takes courage to grow up and be the person you really are."

This chapter concerns a certain young man's rise to meet his Spirit. Because of adversity, he has awakened to his own calling in this world

John wasn't more than 27 or so. He was home when I returned a book I had borrowed from his wife, Carol. John told me he had lost his job a while back. The mine was closing and many had been laid off and he was still out of work. He invited me in and made a pot of coffee for us. I can only relate the following narrative exchange from what I remember, and in reference to the column I wrote about John in the Northern Daily News. John's insight into his own inner self, and his growth is remarkable and also uniquely mature. He was a deep thinker.

They had two sons, Darryl, three, and Danny, about nine months. John had worked underground in one of the local mines.

John tried explaining what it felt like losing his job.

"A person loses more than a job," he said. "I think the loss is also internal, like something inside is gone; a part of who I am. It takes a while to get used to that. It's almost like something inside dies."

Certainly all of us can relate to that from our own life experiences. He went on to say that when we work, we often get so involved with the job that in a sense we "become" that job, instead of being who we are, and who we were meant to be.

I had known John as a serious thinker, who rarely gave his opinion when in a social group, so I was surprised at how talkative he seemed to be on this particular day. Perhaps because I was an adult, and he knew I would listen, he continued, as we sat down for coffee: "You know, with the time I have now, I'm doing some things I've always wanted to do and never had the time for when I had a job. Mind you, I'd still rather be working, have a real job, but what I'm learning, by doing, well maybe someday I'll be able to make use of that."

While we were sitting at the kitchen table, Danny crawled around the table and pulled himself up holding onto John's leg. John continued as he pulled Danny onto his lap, and rumpled his hair: "Power, personal power. I think that's what I'm talking about."

I asked him if personal power meant inner power and he responded, "Maybe it's more than that, maybe it's a sort of spiritual power that I think we all have to one degree or another. Or maybe there's personal power and spiritual power both kind of meshing. All I know is that when you lose your job, you lose power, and it feels awful."

I knew jobs were scarce. Many men had been laid off from the mine that was closing down. I asked John where he had applied for work. He said he was on unemployment insurance, but he had applied for a job in the printing department of the Northern News, but someone else got the job. I saw a flash of disappointment cross his face, before he straightened up and half smiled in a regretful way. He sounded frustrated when he said, "And when you try for another job, your personal power isn't very high. When you don't get the job you try for, then the personal battery goes down and you have to work twice as hard to bring it back up. What is happening to me has something to do with power, but I think I'm slowly developing my own."

I said that I could certainly understand his feelings. My own working path had given me quite a few bumps, now and then, which certainly affected personal power.

He replied, "The new power I am feeling now is a gentler kind of power than when I was working, but I like it better. It's slower growing, but I think it will stay a lot longer." He poured me a second cup and asked, "Remember Ross? He lost his job when I lost mine. But he can't accept the loss and change and he drinks too much. We all used to go out for a beer after work, but the way he drinks now is way too much. I think he is drowning himself in his booze."

John excused himself and went to fetch Darryl, who had awakened from his nap. When he returned, he set Darryl at the kitchen table with us and had crayons and a coloring book ready to share with him. He continued to talk about his life as he colored a bit with Darryl, while I held Danny.

"Me, I've sure learned how hard it is being inside taking care of two kids in diapers all day. But I'm really enjoying my kids. I never knew kids could be so much fun."

I asked him if he played with the kids much, and he laughed. "Kids learn so fast from one day to the next! You know, I always wanted to be a singer. Well, now I am. We all are. We use a broom and mop for microphones, and Danny here, he uses a little hockey stick. We put the tape deck on and howl away." Danny got down from my lap and crawled towards his little hockey stick. John continued, " Somehow, I always feel better after that." Darryl was coloring in his book but looked up at his Dad and said something I didn't understand. John jiggled him, and then put him down.

He continued, "The other night (Darryl) got sick. He was eating a piece of candy and he started to choke. He even started turning blue. I gave him a thump on his back while I held him and that candy went flying across the room. I was so glad I could help him and would have died myself if he hadn't recovered. Being a father is such a responsibility."

Darryl looked back at his dad and grinned.

John talked on in his thoughtful peaceful manner, telling me more about how he felt. He even laughed and said he was talking too much, but felt good talking to an adult. He mentioned that he sure appreciated Carol much more now that he was walking in her footsteps. He talked about how he valued his kids more since he had lost his job. He said that being patient used to be hard for him but the children were teaching him to slow down.

"This time of my life is hard," he continued, "because things are not going the way I want, but there's no sense in crying, and I'm so glad Carol is a real strong woman who has such a positive spirit." He went on to say that he was grateful that at least she was working.

John began to reminisce about his father, describing how his dad used to whittle little figures out of scraps of wood, and made little toys for John and his brothers out of pieces of pipe and anything else he could find. He smiled as he continued, "So he gave me the bug to get busy and do something instead of feeling sorry for myself. "John stood up and beckoned to us all to follow him.

"I want to show you something I've been working on. We can bring the kids with us."

Out in the backyard stood an old wooden grey shed. John opened the creaky door and turned on the light. We all went in and John uncovered something he had put an old towel across.

Reaching out to me from the workbench was a beautiful sculpture in wood of his two children at play.

"I always wanted to work in wood and now I have the time. I guess I never knew how much art was inside me. Working in wood is so soothing and worthwhile. Darryl says I have to make two, one for him and one for his brother. That makes me feel like I really matter, in this old world."

The last time I saw John, he had been hired by a hardware company. The manager told me he really liked the quiet peaceful way John worked, and that he was really good with people. As I left the store John caught up to me, winked and said he got his woodworking tools wholesale, and "that's a real plus!"

As I think back into that memory, I realize John was discovering his own "spiritual gifts" which come to all of us with every adversity, and had moved over to include the Universe in his future.

CHAPTER 11

My Wonderful Parents

The most beautiful thing we can experience is the mysterious -
Albert Einstein

My dad came from Ireland, County Down, near Belfast, where he studied and became an electrical journeyman. Dad came from a family of six children, three boys and three girls. His dad was the chief train engineer for the trains in Belfast which travelled the north and south of Ireland.

Dad's mother had been an opera singer in Belfast and she had made sure that all her children had some sort of training in music. Dad had been given singing lessons and had a "trained bass voice." He read music and sang in our church choir. He made sure we all had music lessons and through his heritage, we all had a strong sense of rhythm and a love of music. Dad fought with the Irish Cavalry in the First World War and rode a horse named Daisy.

After the war, he immigrated to Canada, following his brother Walter. He arrived and worked in the electrical service of a mine in South Porcupine, in northern Ontario, before accepting a position as chief electrician in the Lake Shore Gold Mines in Kirkland Lake. While in South Porcupine, dad met and later married my mother, who was a school teacher. Her name was Laura May Lamb, and they had a family of four children, Margaret, Patricia, Terence and DorisMae.

Dad was not a large man. He used to tell us he was "middle-sized." In Ireland he had been a gymnast, and was in really fine physical shape. He spoke with an Irish brogue, and sang in a wonderful bass voice. When dad sang The Lord's Prayer in church, people would sometimes have tears in their eyes.

His big brown eyes twinkled when he was with us and he teased us gently sometimes, which we loved with all our little hearts. When dad brought out the tool box to fix something, my sister, Margaret, and I followed him around with complete adoration and he would teach us about how and why he was "fixing" whatever. My dad could fix anything!

He wore a tweed cap which I've seen Irishmen wear, along with a dark blue vest over a blue shirt and dark blue pants, all of which were well worn and oil stained. When he came off work he smelled of cigarette smoke and oil from the big electric generators in the mine. When he was going out socially with mom, he wore a grey fedora, a very smart grey suit, white shirt, a tie and black shiny shoes. Then he smelled of Old Spice shaving lotion.

Dad was electrical superintendent of Lake Shore gold mine in Kirkland Lake, Ontario, when the mine opened up in the 1920s and was still there at the request of the mine's new owners around 50 years later to help them close down the mine. He was a very intelligent man. Often, electrical engineers from other local mines, as well as mines as far away as Timmins, Ontario, would come to visit dad at home.

They would describe some problem in the electrical system that was occurring in the workings of their mines. Dad would ask them many questions, and then would say: "Let's talk about something else for awhile." Their conversation would usually be about golf, one of dad's great loves. Just as the golf conversation was getting interesting, dad would hold up his hand and say: "I've got the answer." He would then explain to the visitor what had to be done to unravel the electrical problem in their mines and get things running again. The mine managers of other mines would also send for dad to help them solve an electrical problem in the operation of their mines.

In April, 1972, while taking my mom and my sister, Pat, out for dinner, my dad had a massive stroke which paralyzed him almost completely for 10 months. He died on June 11, 1973, (my sister, Pat's, birthday) at the age of 74.

Mom was a quiet thoughtful lady who loved children, and must have been a good teacher. She came from a family of five children, two boys and three girls. She went to "normal school" as it was called then, to become a teacher. She had received a grant from the government, and worked in northern Ontario to pay it back. She also financed the education of her two younger sisters, one who became a nurse, and the other a secretary. Mom had auburn hair and clear blue eyes that could be piercing when she was after information. She maintained a good weight all her lifetime, and had particularly shapely legs.

Mom was a real "lady", maintaining a placid composure when out, and most of the time when at home. I am very grateful to her for the many dinner conversations which she inspired with her family. Mom made us think by her questions, and to look beyond the situation into the "whys and what makes people do what they do". She would have made a great psychologist.

She had great respect for other people and expected the same in return. She didn't gossip with her neighbors, but maintained a pleasant relationship with everyone. I don't recall that she had any close friends in our neighborhood, but her close friends were women who had been teachers, or who were good church workers, as she was. She had a gentle sense of humor, and warmth for her children which made us tingle with joy, when she beamed at us. Mom could also be tough when it was necessary. Tough in the sense that she would not budge from a high ethical position of moralistic thinking for anyone or anything.

I remember when European men were being sent to our town to work in the mines, after the war. I was in high school at the time and had met three of these men at our teen hangout. One fellow was from Poland, one from Croatia, and I forget where the other was from. They were nice men, who spoke some English. The one from Poland we called "Yank" because he had attached himself to a brigade of American soldiers from Kentucky, and learned his English with a deep southern accent.

I found these men interesting, and brought them all home after school, to meet my mom and have dinner with us. Despite being very surprised, Mom was also very gracious, and cooked up a very fine meal. The men were so grateful and respected mom deeply for her kindness.

I don't know what happened to two of the men, but Yank stayed in Kirkland Lake, and always kept in contact with mom. He helped her out with menial things that needed doing, after dad died, and when she died, he asked to be one of her pallbearers.

My mother had a stroke in 1985 and another one in 1986. I was free to go up and see about her since my 30-year marriage had ended in divorce. She was not well enough to be on her own so I stayed in Kirkland Lake and lived with her.

She was recovering from a stroke and I was there to help her. One evening I went out on a date with a fellow I had known in high school. It was our high-school reunion and many of my friends had come back for the occasion. My friend Joe and I went off to Rouyn, Noranda, across the border into Quebec, and took in a night club show there.

Needless to say, I got home in the wee hours of the morning. As I entered as quietly as I could, there was my mom, sitting straight up in her chair, with blue eyes blazing. "Do you know what time it is young lady?" she asked in her "thunder-and-lightning" voice! I was in my middle 50s at that time. Once a mother, always a mother, I thought to myself. How I loved my mom!

I stayed with mom until her doctor decided she should go into the old-age home, as they called such institutions then. I remember that day clearly because we both went home in shock, after the doctor made that decision. When we returned home after the doctor's visit, mom pulled out a brand new box of Laura Secord chocolates someone had given her, from her bureau. We both sat down and ate the whole box. We both knew it was time for her to move since she had begun to wander the house at night when I was working and had dumped a hot kettle on the floor and slipped in the water. I stayed on in Kirkland Lake so that I could visit her daily and I decided I would probably spend the rest of my life in Kirkland Lake, so I bought a house on Duncan Avenue. The year was 1989.

My little home was nestled between two high hills. I had put a lot of love into my house. A very talented carpenter by the name of Al Dumas was hired to finish the basement and electricians brought the electrical system up to par. Plumbers had installed a lovely, big bathtub, the kind with jets and bubbles beside the washroom in the basement.

I loved to have a nice bath, with candles and nice aromas to help me relax. In the rest of the basement the electricians put in a gas fireplace, with granite rocks as a mantle. (They called my new basement a "play room".)

At the bottom of the stairs on the right was another room which I later called "the pump room." It had storage shelves and I used the room for extra equipment I had brought up from the south, in hopes of starting a business. Along the cement floor in the hallway about 10 feet from the "pump room" was a drain embedded in the cement floor.

I worked as nursing supervisor on nights in Extendicare, which was a large facility for taking care of the chronically ill.

It seemed to me that it had been raining for weeks, and it was around the end of April when most of the snow had melted and the spring air was coming in. I remember coming off duty and thinking how tiresome was the rain, and how steady the downpour.

As usual, I went to bed shortly after I got home, after first having my bath in that wonderful tub, watching the flickering flames in the gas fireplace.

I was deep asleep in my bed upstairs when someone shook me gently on my shoulder. I was the only one living in my house, and had locked all the doors carefully before getting into bed. However, for some reason I was not alarmed and turned to see who was waking me up.

It was my dad. He beckoned me to get up and through telepathy told me to go down to the basement. As I descended the stairs, I saw with horror that there was water coming towards me on the floor. It was creeping up the hall from the drain in the cement floor just in front of the door to my "playroom." Dad sent me into the "pump room" and beckoned me towards an old contraption on the floor. He said: "Jiggle that silver wire." I did as he asked and the pump roared into action. Soon, the water drained away.

I turned to thank my dad, but he was gone.

Dad had always looked out for us all when he was alive. I know this experience was not just a figment of my imagination. Dad probably knew how important that little finished room was to me. It was the creative development of me as a single person again, and the first tender shoots of a new beginning. I now was taking care of just me for a change.

Mom was still alive when this happened. When I told her of the incident she was not at all surprised. She said dad had come to her when she was mounting the stairs in the old house, walking up the stairs behind her. He had sat on their bed beside her and said to her: "I'm so lonely for you." Then he disappeared. When mom told me that, it made me realize that Spirits on the other side of the curtain feel every emotion that we all do on this side of life.

Dad helped me preserve the new renovations in my little basement. He always respected my creativity and gave me encouragement. He also must have known I had spent almost my last cent on that new beginning.

I believe, and also know from many experiences, that people who have graduated to the Heavenly Kingdom are not gone, because they visit us frequently and help out if and when necessary. Isn't life a wonderful mystery!

Love never stops. It emanates from the kingdom higher than ours, leading, guiding and protecting us. I know our own lives never stop because my Dad was as genuine in Spirit as he had been when he was my earthly dad. Praise the Lord for Love.

CHAPTER **12**

The Spirited Round Table of Senior Discussions

As we listen to and observe other people, we glimpse their countless different worlds —the worlds of experiences they have journeyed through and accumulated in their lives. - DorisMae Honer

Queen Elizabeth visited Ottawa sometime in June or July of 1992, to celebrate Canada's 125th anniversary since Confederation. She had come for three days. Her visit was well publicized and the preparation for the event was great.

During her visit, there was one unusual event which disrupted the rather placid news coverage of her visit, and was definitely not a planned event for a royal visitor.

The newscast reported that a group of young women had staged a parade and were stopped before they got to the place where the queen was to make an appearance.

In the early 1990's a group of women described in the media as a grassroots feminist orientation movement was forming in Canada. The services and activities of the movement were aimed at increasing the options and choices available to women with the goal of promoting self-determination and autonomy.

Although this specific parade of women was reported because of their general appearance, they were not identified at that time as being part of any specific women's group. It was reported that their parade had been stopped by police because the women were topless.

Perhaps the parading women were a small splinter group of some new feminist group with their own agenda, and certainly ill advised in their partial nakedness. Although I have searched the Ottawa newspapers, I have not found any traces of this event. Perhaps it was squashed. However, in 1992, it was big news on the local radios. The following little story relates how some senior women accepted the news.

In the nursing home in Kirkland Lake, Ontario, there were a small group of ladies who had joined together daily in the lounge at about 3 p.m. to socialize. These precious senior ladies were sitting by the window having a cup of tea. I was working afternoons at the time and could overhear their conversation.

The sun rested on Maude's shoulder and made a halo of her white hair as she spoke.

"I've never heard of such a misuse of energy!" she exclaimed. "Imagine all those young women marching in a parade so they can take off their shirts and walk bare breasted through town!"

Angela started to giggle. Now before we go any further, let me describe Angela. She stood about five feet with about a size 48 bust line. She was 78 years young.

"Well," she said with a big twinkle, "if I was out there with those young folk, and took off my brassiere, I'd probably hit all those gawkers in the eye and knock 'em out cold!"

Mary leaned into the group over her tea cup: "Looks like you might be a secret weapon, Angela."

The ladies noticed me as I was passing by and one held out her hand to stop and include me in the conversation. "Tell me, DorisMae, would you go parading around bare-chested like those women reported in the news?"

Before I could even think, Angela pointed at me and squealed: "Oh she's another secret weapon from the looks of her!"

We all had a good laugh, and then giggled some more as

Gertrude said: "I just don't understand the point of it all. Surely women of today have more to occupy their minds than wanting to go bare from the waist up, and as you know, Ottawa can be mighty chilly even in the summer, especially if it rains."

Mary, having settled back in her chair after our humorous exchange, added thoughtfully: "Why, in my day we were so busy rolling bandages, knitting socks, helping the kids with their homework, being nurse, doctor, counselor, gardener, volunteer, teacher and a lot more. We didn't have the time to think of such trivial matters."

Anna was winding up for a comment. Anna had come to Canada from Europe years ago, with her husband who had signed up to work in the mines. She had learned some English but with a very heavy accent. Her grammar was often a little distorted. She had the greatest sense of humor. We all loved her and were smiling because we knew she would say something very down to earth and also hilarious. Anna snorted. "They be crazy down south there. Not so crazy up here in the north. Girls going out up here, all bare like that, all they get is fly-bitten and maybe boob droop!"

Olga had just come to join us and remarked: "'I hope the world knows those young and probably flat-bosomed young women do not represent the majority of Canadian women. I think they are a very small minority. In my time, this kind of thinking would not have even been considered. We were so glad when that airplane inventor (Howard Hughes) invented the brassiere for that buxom actress, what was her name? I can't remember like I used to." Olga was quiet for a moment trying to remember. (The name of the actress was Jane Russell.)

Anna chimed in: "Here in Kirkland Lake, lots of women are big breasted. Ever notice that? Maybe it's something in the water. Say, maybe we should be smart and open a business, and sell our water to all those young girls. Then maybe they be thinking better!"

The sun had gone down, as I passed by once more on my rounds. Angela had fallen asleep; Mary had left to meet her daughter; and Anna's book lay half closed on her lap as she dozed. I looked at these wonderful northern women, and felt such a rush of joy and love for them. They had paid their dues, faced the harsh realities of life, and survived. They knew how to sift life's importance from its trivialities. As I walked softly away, Angela opened one eye.

"Now DorisMae, don't you be going knocking anybody's eye out."

I turned to reply: "Not me, Angela," but she was snoring gently.

CHAPTER 13

The Canadian Health-Care System

Oh Canada...
with glowing hearts
we see thee rise,
the true north strong and free.
From the Canadian National Anthem.

This next little story is about what the small group of seniors in the nursing home thought about the Canadian health-care system.

There were six of them. They were all grey or white haired; courageous ladies all who had suffered various disabilities, none of which impaired their thinking processes.

They had begun to meet regularly around one of the tables in the sitting room. The year was 1993, in the northern Ontario town of Kirkland Lake.

"I'm confused," said Mary, "we're in an economic recession, yet we, the taxpayers, are spending more and more money on health care and we are all living on less income. As seniors, our income is fixed . . . and the politicians seem more interested in giving themselves raises rather than increasing our old-age pensions. The amount that is being spent on health care is terrible! People are abusing the privilege and we all pay for that abuse!"

Anna was next to give her opinion. Anna speaks in a heavily accented way. She came to Canada from Europe as an adult but gets along just fine. She is very down to earth and has a great sense of humor, as well as a very down to earth outlook on life.

"All I ever got was medicine," sniffed Anna. "I don't speak so good English. Anyway, I only got sick when Joe gave me the worries. After he die, no more worries, no more sick. Those pills the doctor gave me made me slow and sleepy. I couldn't see right either, so I throw them away in the garbage."

Olga leaned forward as she shuffled the cards: "I wonder how many people drain our health-care system by dwelling on their aches and pains?" She cut the deck, shuffled again and began to deal the cards. She continued: "I've found in my own life that the more I dwell on something, the bigger it gets. If I am thinking on how sick I feel, I seem to get sicker. So I've learned to ignore aches and pains and am feeling much better now!"

Angela picked up the cards and examined her hand: "I've given up smoking girls, and I'm hungry all the time, but I'm darned if I will give my grandson second-hand smoke and make him sick with cancer."

The ladies played their hands thoughtfully, and the deck was passed back to Mary who shuffled and then dealt the cards in another round. She dealt her first card as she said thoughtfully: "Our health-care system seems to be a reasonable service, but in actuality, we are paying not only for legitimate expenses, but also for many people's poor health habits, and encouraging them to keep their bad habits by paying for their medical expenses. Their bad habits propel them into illnesses." Mary was an American lady married to a Canadian.

"(The Canadian) health-care system is better than the one in the US, where insurance companies have their own set of rules. For example, if a person has been sick too long the insurance company simply will discharge that person and refuse to pay any more."

"They also won't insure a person if they have certain diseases, or even if they have been born with pre-existing problems. They seem to be able to charge whatever they want to and discharge a person if they think that person is costing them too much money; never mind how much the person has paid into their system. It's terrible and no one is doing anything about it!"

Anna was fidgeting, and then blurted out: "So maybe we should pay the people who help us stay well. Maybe instead of pills we give out prescriptions for exercise and better health habits." Anna looked like a little elf with a white dandelion crown. "Anyway, come on girls, let's play cards. I danced with Frank at the Encore Club last week. I told him I no kiss him 'till he stops smoking. Last night he told me he quit and we gonna meet today, at three o'clock. Let's play cards so I don't miss my date!"

After thinking of these ladies and their conversation, I realized how fortunate we are in Canada to have a health care plan that helps all of us. When in the United States, where I stay for about five and a half months each winter, I interviewed Dr. Gregory Porter, my family doctor there.

Dr. Porter explained some of the problems as he saw them.

"First of all, no health-insurance company should have the right to terminate anyone because their illness is costing the company too much money," and he added, "That is heartless."

"No one should be refused health-insurance coverage because of congenital problems. There is also way too much paperwork. The insurance forms all need to be simplified."

Dr. Porter was itemizing his thoughts and mentioned that there should be significant emphasis on prevention.

"Foods should be monitored and the salt, sugar and amount of preservatives need to be addressed. If you read all the ingredients which make up canned and packaged foods, it's no wonder we have obesity and diabetes running rampant in this country. Cheap food contains way too much of all that and it's the poor people who suffer."

Dr. Porter continued:

"We need a more educated public. We need to spend much more on teachers who will educate the public on healthy eating habits. A public which is better educated will be a public with far less obesity and childhood diabetes."

He also contended that Type 2 diabetes (or adult-onset diabetes) can be prevented.

"Prevention of Type 2 Diabetis would cut down on medical expenses and I'll bet it would also cut down on crime. Better education, and better knowledge regarding food gives people more breaks in society. Good healthy food makes people feel better."

Dr. Porter went on to say that people need to be encouraged to walk and exercise as well as eat better. "I take aim at all the couch potatoes and car addicts," he added. "Their lack of real exercise is killing (them)." The phone rang again, this time an emergency in St. Mary's hospital.

While he stood up and fumbled for his keys he commented, "Finally, tort reform is needed to set limits on suing doctors. Doctors are so hesitant to treat a patient without using a barrage of expensive tests because they feel they the need to protect themselves from lawsuits."

Discussions about health care are often heard whenever people get together. Change and improvements are coming and we welcome the time when prevention is as every bit as important as the treatments of existent illnesses.

CHAPTER 14

Night Dive

You've got to find the force inside of you - Joseph Campbell

That night was darker than usual. Brooding black clouds covered the moon as we put on our wet suits and equipment for the final scuba dive of the night. We were told to check our underwater flashlights carefully.

Eskar Park beach, where we met, was illuminated by a gas light the dive master had put on a folding table. He gave us our instructions and assigned our dive buddies.

There was a surplus of male divers so I was given two tall, broad-shouldered men as my partners.

Joe was about six feet tall, lean and muscular. He seemed nervous, talking fast and moving in a jerky, tense manner.

Benny was a little shorter, and husky with a barrel chest. His legs looked like tree trunks. His manner was more laid back and when he talked his voice was smooth and quiet.

The lake was calm as we entered and I noticed how soft and mushy the bottom was. We were to complete certain maneuvers and then come back to shore where our dive master was waiting to check us back in.

My dive partners were strong swimmers. Standing just under five feet, I did not expect to match their pace.

As we completed the maneuvers, I began to lag behind and then my flashlight went out. At the same time I realized my buoyancy device wasn't working and I was beginning to sink.

I thought I could push myself up from the bottom and surface, so I didn't worry. I had forgotten our dive master's warning that we were not to touch the lake bottom.

I kept sinking through something that was not just water. It felt like soft, silky mud. I kept banging my flashlight and finally it connected and shone again. I struggled to get out from the sucking silt and kept getting pulled down deeper. Fear crept over me.

What was I to do? "Unlock your weight belt and let it go," said a clear voice within me. "No," I answered in the stupor of creeping cold shock. "I just finished paying off the huge cost of my equipment."

"Then you had better pray," came the answer from within. (If I had detached my weight belt, my own buoyancy would have made it easier to possibly swim up to the surface.)

Two flashlights were approaching. It was Joe and Benny! They pulled me from the bottom and when we surfaced I began to hyperventilate. Fear had overcome my ability to breathe normally. I heard myself making loud gasping sounds and could do nothing to stop it.

When we neared the shore, the dive master took over. He stripped off my buoyancy device vest and I heard him swear loudly and yell: "This isn't working! It's stuck!" Benny stayed with me, reassuring me, and eventually I got control of my breathing.

"You hit the bottom called loon shit," my instructor shouted hoarsely. "It's like sinking into quick sand. Lucky you had two partners."

Benny said: "We thought you were with us and when we couldn't see your flashlight we surfaced to find you, thinking you had surfaced too. When we didn't see you, we both went back. We figured you were in trouble. We're glad we found you!" He took a breath and put a strong arm around me and kept me gripped in a big hug.

When I stopped shaking and regained my calm, my instructor put another buoyancy device vest on me and ordered me back into the water. Benny said he would come with me. We were to swim across to a floating raft and surface, wave at the instructor and dive once more, all at about 20 feet down.

If the instructor had not made me dive that night for the second time I might never have found the nerve to go down again. Since we had passed all the requirements of the test, we all received our certificates.

The store manager who had sold me the equipment was incredulous since it was top-of-the-line gear. Sure enough, there was a glitch in the valve, which they fixed. The flashlight was replaced.

I dove several times after that, always with other big strong divers as my "dive buddies" and always in a group. In Mexico I discovered that those huge six-foot fish called groupers would make squealing noises when we fed them.

Once off Maui, we dove to a coral formation standing about 25 feet high, which was called an underwater cathedral. It was shaped in a curved sphere, with the sides open like large oval-shaped windows. While I knelt in the center on a small flat rock, looking up, I watched bright colored fish swim in and out of the cathedral windows as the sunshine streamed down through turquoise waters.

When diving off the Barbados I knelt on the firm sandy bottom and watched a "man o' war" – a jelly-like invertebrate marine animal - swim above me. I've swum with huge turtles more than 100 years old, in bright, clear waters, always staying within 30 feet of the surface where visibility is best. On recreation dives I never went deeper.

The underwater natural world moves more slowly and quietly than our world. However, there are dangerous currents in the ocean which can sweep a diver away in a second. Under the Great Lakes there are ocean liners with engines so powerful that their resounding underwater "clicking" sounds can make tooth fillings rattle like flamenco dancers inside a diver's mouth.

On each dive, I think it was God who made sure my dive partners were strong men.

It has been 19 years since I took my last dive, but my memories of those dives are as clear as those beautiful bright sunny days when diving was such a pleasure, and that one black fearsome night when God and two angels (Joe and Benny) protected me from my own foolishness, and made it possible that I'm still here today.

CHAPTER **15**

The Many Spirits Involved in a Special Secret

Slow down and enjoy life. It's not the scenery you miss by going too fast—you also miss the sense of where you are going, and why - Eddie Cantor, American comedian

The receptionist at the Empress Hotel in Victoria, British Columbia, Canada, was very co-operative. Full of excitement, I had asked to speak to the manager and, after a few questions, she put me through. The manager listened intently as I told him I wanted to give Ray, my husband, a real surprise birthday party. He was delighted to be in on the "secret."

We agreed on massages in the spa room, dinner in the hotel's Bengal room restaurant and an overnight stay in one of their rooms. Then the next day, before we checked out, we were to enjoy the hotel's famous "High Tea." It was going to be a real party; and it would be a secret!

The Empress Hotel is a wonderful old building in the Edwardian, chateau style. It was designed by Francis Rattenbury for Canadian Pacific Hotels as a terminal hotel for Canadian Pacific's steamship line. It was built between 1904 and 1908 and they added wings in 1909, and again in 1914 and 1928.

This Hotel is the pride of the people in Victoria, British Columbia. It has played hostess to kings and queens, movie stars and many other famous people.

In 1989, restoration took place at a cost of $40 million, with the goal to restore the hotel to its pre-war elegance. One of the famous offerings of the Empress is its afternoon "High Tea" which is a classic Edwardian tea served with sandwiches, fresh scones, fruit preserves and Jersey cream with the tea.

It was November 23 and time to set the plan in motion. Ray's birthday is the 24th and he had no idea where we were going as we packed and headed for downtown Victoria. As we neared the hotel, I told him we were going to the Empress.

"You are kidding of course," he said. "No," I answered. "We're going into the Empress Hotel. It's all arranged. It's your birthday present."

When we arrived at the registration desk, the sweet receptionist said: "Oh yes, we've been expecting you." After signing in, we were taken to our room by a bellhop and told that the spa appointment was at 2:30 p.m.

What a beautiful experience that was. First we soaked in a pool filled with herbs which had a heavenly scent. Then we were given big fluffy bathrobes and led to a room subtly lit, with a fireplace on one wall throwing warm, friendly light into the room.

Music came from somewhere and was quiet and relaxing. There were two massage tables set up, side by side, and two massage therapists waiting. The massages were heavenly and we relaxed into blissful and healing quietness.

After our massages, we had about an hour to wait for the dinner reservation in the Bengal room, famous for its curry buffet. I was excited when we entered that lovely room. It was crowded with people standing around holding drinks and chatting spiritedly to each other.

The waiter, however, was a little anxious about the revelry and increasing noise. Apparently there was a convention of salespeople ongoing and they had come to the Bengal room for drinks before dinner. When we attempted to approach the buffet table we were blocked by the salespeople who simply didn't see us, in their socializing with each other. Our waiter was more than anxious on our return with empty hands. He brought us drinks "on the house."

I was fascinated with the interactions of the sales group and also somewhat amused. However, our waiter was not. We had a good view of the archway on the far wall and suddenly there appeared there a man in uniform, who seemed more than six feet tall and wide across the shoulders. He was fully armed it seemed and as he leaned against one side of the arch way, with his muscular arms crossed and his eyes boring keenly into the sales crowd, a gradual hush came over the room.

Then the salespeople scurried for their tables and sat down. The quiet music was again heard by all in the room. The man in the archway (he was part of the hotel's security team) straightened up, smiled at the room, turned and left. Not a word had been spoken by that security officer.

Although the Bengal room did not offer floor shows, that was, nevertheless, the best reality "floor show" we had ever witnessed!

The next morning we were to check out after we had High Tea.

What a sampling of different delicately rolled sandwiches and scones that was. I had whispered to the head maitre d' that it was Ray's birthday, and, smiling, he said: "I know. It's a secret isn't it?"

Suddenly, we heard the tinkle of "Happy Birthday" from the pianist there and the waiter brought a chocolate cupcake with a candle in it.

It was such a fitting end to the "birthday secret" in the Empress Hotel.

The Spirit of Joy which the Empress manager and employees gave us is eternal in our memories and Ray still talks about it as if it was only yesterday.

CHAPTER **16**

The Spirits of Charlie and Ginny

Learn to get in touch with the silence within yourself and know that everything in this life has a purpose - Elizabeth Kubler-Ross

The year was 1997. The little furry cream-colored fellow was six weeks old at the time. He and his brother and sister were brought out and placed on the floor for us to examine. The female was already sold. The males were both blondish, with tints of caramel.

One of the males opened his eyes and began to crawl towards us. He was so tiny he couldn't really walk yet, but he tried so hard and he made it to Bryan and me, and put his little head on my foot. What could I do but pick him up and love him. He had chosen us.

My husband, Bryan, was chronically ill and knew that his health was running out. He had been told by his doctors that he should put all his affairs in order. One day he had said to me: "What would you like, a cat or a dog?" I replied that a cat would be easier to take care of and he scratched his head and then replied: "I'm damned if I'm going to be replaced by a cat! Let's look for a poodle puppy."

That's how Charlie, my miniature poodle, and I met, and he remained with me for almost 10 years.

Charlie earned his flight wings when he was about 12 weeks old. I put him in a flight carrier bag for small dogs, and he never made a peep - or a woof - while he was under the plane's seat in front of me. As long as he could see my feet, he was quiet. No one ever knew he was on board until we were getting ready to disembark. I had Charlie in his carrier bag over my shoulder when a little boy spotted him through the carrier's screen and said in a loud voice: "Oh, look at the doggie!!"

Then everyone around me had to "look at the doggie." Bryan called him "Prince Charles" because I loved that little ball of fluff so much. His little tail would wag so fast I thought he would take off.

When Bryan died, it was a terrible loss for me, and Charlie was a great comfort. He seemed to know when my heart was breaking with grief and loneliness. He would jump up into my lap and he would snuggle and keep me warm and loved. He was such a gift.

As time went on, I went back to school and began socializing. Charlie was really fussy about who I brought home, especially if it was a man. My friend, Ray, was the only fellow he wagged his tail at and allowed in for any reason. Ray became a close friend, and later friendship blossomed into love.

Ray and I were married in 2000. Charlie loved Ray. He would put his little head on Ray's thigh when we were all driving along in the truck on a long trip and go to sleep. However, if Ray put on a signal light Charlie would be up looking out the window to see why we were slowing down or turning. He was a great traveler.

Once, we put his airline carrier on the bed and I opened it to prepare it for another flight. The phone rang and I went to answer it. Later we realized that Charlie was not around. We called, but there was no answer. We looked all over for him and finally spotted him inside the dog carrier which I had left on the bed unzipped. He didn't wish to be left behind.

Charlie had quite a personality. When we had company, he would go to each person and wag his tail before bringing out his toys to show everyone.

When we went for a walk, he would walk on my left side, and heel - usually. Sometimes, Charlie would "take Ray for a walk."

One morning Charlie raced out to the side room and started barking furiously. He was making such a racket that Ray went after him to see what was going on. Outside the window, where Charlie had stationed himself, were two young dark-skinned teenagers who had crept into our park and were trying to steal a neighbor's golf cart.

When they saw us in the window, they used the golf cart as a stepping booster to haul themselves over a barbed wire fence. Charlie had done a good job of warning us.

Charlie came with us everywhere we could take him. In Victoria, British Columbia, where we live part time, I stayed behind to finish a course I was taking in school, while Ray returned to Tucson. Our British Columbia home was in the mountains and I enjoyed a lovely walk each day on the back trail going up to the saw mill. Apparently I was not the only one who was familiar with the trail.

One night I worked late and just as I was turning in to go to bed, Charlie went steaming back into the sunroom barking up a storm. We had sliding doors onto the back deck and Charlie was snarling and guarding that door with his sharp white teeth bared in a nasty snarl.

Outside the door was a man looking intently into the porch. When he saw Charlie, and then me with the phone at my ear, he disappeared down the trail. The police came almost immediately, but could find no trace of him in the forest, although they did a really thorough check. Charlie was my hero and had saved me again.

When travelling once from Minnesota to Victoria, we drove through South Dakota and arrived in a town called Sturgis during the annual motorcycle rally. Ray went to get some oil for the car. All the stations were glutted with motorcycles and there were bikes everywhere.

When Charlie wants to see something in the distance he will rise up on his hind legs and walk upright. He was looking up the hill for Ray at the gas station and he was walking on two legs. He remained that way, concentrating on what Ray was doing, and unaware of the attention he was attracting from the bikers across the road from where we were standing.

I saw that he had gained quite an audience, so I scooped Charlie up and we both took a bow. The bikers all applauded with great friendly laughs and clapping hands.

Charlie was also a great nurse. In 2007, I became really sick with shingles. It was so bad it infected my spinal cord, the rash stretching from my sternum right back to the spine. Charlie stayed on my bed faithfully, never leaving except to relieve himself. He was my angel nurse.

When I started to get better and was able to walk, he walked right beside me. When I fell, he whined and licked my face, trying to help me get back on my feet. He definitely understood my pain and was right there to help me.

The years rolled along and Ray and I had Charlie with us almost all the time.

He loved music, mostly the quieter music, but in his early years he would dance jive on his hind legs with me. He had become, through the years, a protector, nurse, sleuth, compassionate loving companion and playmate that possessed a good sense of humor and a very kind heart.

On Jan. 7, 2009, Charlie had a terrible accident. Our vet did all she could to help Charlie. She made arrangements for Charlie to be admitted to a special veterinary clinic in Tucson, which provided 24-hour service. We took him there that evening and visited him twice daily.

Charlie was holding his own despite the entire trauma, until he got pneumonia.

Despite all the treatment and tender loving care that he received, there, Charlie's little body could not keep up and he was ready to go to the next kingdom on Feb. 3. We loved him enough to very reluctantly let him go.

Words do not ever describe the ongoing pain which literally consumed both Ray and I. Oh, we kept on with all the things that had to be done on the plane of the living, but we missed him daily and life developed a big hole in it for both of us.

I wrote a letter of thanks to the veterinary clinic, and added to it two poems I had written since Charlie's death. Grief is an extremely painful emotion, whether the loss be human or animal. I tried to describe it through this poem.

GRIEF...

I think grief has many colors.
Sometimes it is silver grey.
That's when a person has to
go out into society and
wear an acceptable face.
Other times, when one is alone
and grief is fresh; its color is dark navy blue,
with shards of slimy green and black mixed in,
and stabbing flashes of red hot anger too.
These colors make our insides feel rotten with pain.
Grief also manufactures tears that taste salty.
Tears wash through the excruciating pain
sometimes bringing rays of white light.

As time goes on grief fades.
Is it because life's sunlight pushes grief into the past?
But unresolved grief never goes away.
It just gets smaller, and older,
hiding painfully someplace inside us,
like in arthritis or some other illness,
until one day, grief dies.
I suppose that's because we die too and fly away.

A Day After Forever......

I guess letting go of a loved one,
who has passed to the next life,
whether they be a human or a pet,
in losing them, it's really hard and painful.
Now I ask you, "How do we let go of
dark intelligent eyes, a wiggle waggle tail
and a warm Charlie body full of loving snuggles?"
We treated our little one who died as if
he was going to be with us FOREVER,
and maybe . . .a day after that.
We never looked ahead to the time
he would leave us, and go
far beyond our reach.
What terrible thoughts jump into
the darkest corners of our minds,
like endless accusing drums, beating
rhythms of "I should have; or I should not have,"
driving pain deeper into our sobbing, tormented souls.
A wise teacher friend said it in one word.
"Remorse. You have to deal with remorse."

Remorse is colored deep purple and gold,
like sunsets, when day is dying,
and again, more gently painted
in soft newborn Dawns.
If sunsets are another way of seeing Remorse,
then tell me, "What is Dawn?
Is Dawn another way of change overcoming Remorse?
Of moving into Growth and Resolution?"

Purples and golds are also the colors of majesty,
sung musically by deep, warm tenor and bass Spirit Voices.
Their songs help us to heal, to remember the good times,
the funny things that made us laugh,
to celebrate our loved one's life,
to remember their many ways,
and keep their little paw prints
safely, lovingly printed in our hearts.

Softly, slowly and gently, I begin to see Dawn.
It breaks like the sun's warming rays
through those blue black clouds of Grief.
Loved ones are part of our reason for BEING.
An ancient truth I learn over and over again.
I know that Charlie's life's task is done.
He lived and died with Love and Honor.
"Wait now," the Spirits command,
"Stand up! Well done! We know you did your BEST!"
"We place these purple and golden robes of majesty
with great respect and blessings upon your Inner Selves.
Now go forth with Love, Trust and Faith!"

Charlie, my little one, thank you
for all the many beautiful times we both
shared together on our journey.
Dawn breaks softly on this new day.
I guard your loving Spirit gently, carefully
safely in my heart, until one day in the future
when my own life tasks are done,
we will meet again, you and I,
in a far better place, FOREVER,
and maybe even . . . A Day after That.
February 2009

Ginny, a loving Spirit:

Every blade of grass has its angel that bends over it and whispers "grow, grow" - The Talmud

My son, Robert, was very concerned at our loss of Charlie and asked me if I wanted to take his little dog, Ginny. She is a very cute three-year-old poodle cross. Rob said he and his wife, Linda, work all day and go to bed fairly early and Ginny doesn't have much time to be with the family. Rob's children come to visit him on the weekends and at other times convenient to Rob and his first wife Jennifer. They love to play with Ginny, but they were concerned about her too.

Little Hope, Rob's youngest, had a great bond with Ginny and it was tough for her to let little Ginny go. But Hope has such a big heart for a little girl, and she said to me: "Grandma, I want you to take Ginny. I'll miss her, but we have a dog at my other home, and I want Ginny to go to a good home where she can run and play."

Everyone wanted the best for Ginny.

For a while, Ginny had become partially paralyzed for reasons no one knew for sure. Her vet said that sometimes dogs with long backs have spinal problems. Ginny loved to jump high, and sometimes she falls off furniture onto the floor. Perhaps she struck and damaged her back in a fall.

In losing Charlie, Ray and I were very sad and the kids insisted we fly out and get to know Ginny. Her real name is Gin Seng, but to everyone around us she is Ginny.

Perhaps Ginny's dad was a beagle because when she barks it is more like a beagle on the hunt. She is tiny, with little short legs and a fairly long body. Her head - and her intelligence - is more like a poodle. And her hair is, too. She has big brown eyes, curly cream colored fur which is like Charlie's, and although Charlie was very bright, we both think Ginny is even smarter.

She is inquisitive, loving and manipulative, and has Ray wrapped right around her little paw. She is very protective of both Ray and I and because of this we are taking her to doggie school so that she can get used to what we expect, and let go of some of her habits of wanting to protect us from the world.

When we met Ginny, she could walk, run and jump a little, but she was still incontinent in the house at times, which was a residue of her paralysis. For that reason Rob had been advised to keep her in a pen when he and Linda were working, and also at night to sleep. Rob was very concerned that she was in the pen too much, and therefore was willing to give her up, so that she could have a more stimulating life.

The flight back to British Columbia was not too easy for little Ginny. However, we all made it without too many problems and Ginny settled into our mountain home as if she had always been there.

Ginny loves to run and play fetch, and we bought her many different toys. She prefers the soft ones which she can lift up in her mouth. However, she also adopted a teddy bear and a stuffed bob cat kitten of mine, and since they are almost bigger than she is, she initially used them to dust mop my floors as she pushes them ahead of her around our home. Now she can lift them and jump up to her favorite spot on Ray's chair, or the couch.

When she is in pursuit of something and stops suddenly, her backside doesn't stop with her front paws, and she goes rolling over. It never phases her, and she has more energy now that a puppy.

On occasion, she limps a little when she first gets up to walk or run and we figure that's a remnant of the fall she must have sustained which resulted in the paralysis she had a while ago. Her incontinence has completely cleared up and we let her out often so that she has no accidents in the house. She also lets us know when she needs to go out.

We take her for her "spa" treatments (bath, clip, nails, ears and lamb's cut) about every six weeks. She has completely charmed our vet and the girls at the groomers. When she sees them, she squints at them and licks their hands with her soft, warm tongue. Everyone loves her.

Ginny's little Spirit has repaired to a great degree the big empty hole that Charlie's death brought to our lives. We will always keep Charlie's memory alive in our hearts. Love never dies, and we know Charlie is now liberated from pain and running free in the next kingdom, waiting for us to come home. When Robert came to visit, Ginny was ecstatic with joy and love, and Robert kept teasing me that Ginny now looked too much like a poodle and he offered to give her a "Rob's haircut". No thank you, Ginny is just beautiful the way she is now.

Both Charlie and Ginny have such loving Spirits. Thank you, God, for blessing us.

CHAPTER **17**

Three Courageous and Very Special Spirits

With the gift of listening, comes the healing - Catherine de Hueck
(writer, pioneer for social justice.)

My granddaughter, Hope, and I were discussing the importance of having an education in the fields we are most drawn to. At this point Hope has said she will be a vet as she is a great animal lover. However, she is young and has just landed a wonderful role in a play. Apparently she won the part hands down, so her passions may change. I want her to know how pursuing more education will open up new experiences in her life. It certainly has in my life. I want her to know that education is a wonderful journey in itself.

Some of the people I met and experiences I had are so precious to me, when I was working towards my degree, and did my two internships at Prescott College, in Arizona.

I was working towards a bachelor of arts with a major in recreational art for special populations.

"What is that, Grandma?" Hope asked.

"Well, it is something like using the arts, music, painting, writing, sculpture and plain creating as recreation tools to help people get better, instead of people dwelling on their aches and pains," I explained.

In the next three stories, I have changed the names of both the facility, and my clients.

Julia: ━━━━━━━━━━━━━━━━━━━━━━━

The life that is not examined is not worth living - Plato

Julia was a patient is the Santa Marta Chronic Care Facility and was considered a very difficult person to understand. She heaved books, flower vases, and verbal insults at the nurses and any staff who wished to enter her room. Her wild temper was famous throughout the building, and people tiptoed past her room in order to avoid any raucous outbursts. (Although she was considered a difficult patient, all the Santa Marta staff was very kind to her, and gave her excellent nursing care.) In odd comparison to the loud bursts of energy, and curses like a truck driver, Julia was a tiny woman with huge brown eyes in a heart-shaped, pixie-like face.

Julia had MS (multiple sclerosis). The name multiple sclerosis means "many scars," which is characterized by many scars and/or lesions in the spinal column and brain. Symptoms include vision problems, extreme fatigue, muscle stiffness, weakness, poor balance, tingling - usually in extremities - often including bowel and bladder problems and depression.

Judy was the administrator. Judy is a very kind and compassionate woman whom I am lucky to count as my friend. She phoned me in desperation and asked if I could work with Julia. The year was 2001, and I was in school working towards my degree. I decided to use the Santa Marta Chronic Care facility as one of my internships.

When Julia and I first met, she was confined to her bed, and once in awhile a wheel chair. Julia had also been given another diagnosis, that of bipolar disorder.

The first encounter with her was quite surprising. One of the nurses warned that she would "probably cuss your ears off." She related in great detail of the dire consequences of even trying to enter her room. It was somewhat alarming to say the least. Cautiously, I knocked at Julia's doorway even though her door was wide open. A lady as tiny as a 10-year-old child turned angry eyes in my direction: "What do you want?" she asked.

"May I come in?" I asked. She seemed surprised. Julia fixed me with bold eyes: "All right, you can come in. Now what do you want?" she demanded again.

"I need your help," I explained.

"How can I help you?" she asked, less defensively and more interested.

I explained that I was starting an internship at her nursing home as a student of Prescott College and was working towards a degree in recreation. She asked more questions about the program and then agreed that she would be one of my clients.

During that initial interview, Julia mentioned she liked music and art, liked people reading to her, wanted short stories, some from the bible, and maybe some poetry. Julia remarked, "I can't get up any more, to get my hair done, and it's hard to put on makeup."

Continuing, she added: "Although a lot of people don't think I am a spiritual person, I really am. I love to go to church, and I am not fussy what church I attend, I just like to go."

Julia said she wanted some spiritual work done but not now, maybe later. She continued to tell me what she liked and didn't like. "I don't like movies or TV, but I love bright colors. I used to enjoy cooking too, but my world has gotten so small."

One of the programs which evolved from our first meeting included poetry reading, story reading, puppets, music, art and making a tapestry. We named the plan a "Three Part Program" at Julia's suggestion.

We met in Julia's room every Tuesday morning for 30 minutes to an hour, depending on Julia's condition that particular day. The goal of the program was to stimulate Julia's interest in activities, and to increase her self esteem.

The objectives mapped out for her were the following: an introduction to, and manipulation of, hand puppets. We included also reading and writing poems. The third project would be making a tapestry. Julia wished to choose all the tapestry colors, since she loved color. We would use music in the background of all activities.

The equipment needed was the following: A CD player and quiet CD's, (Julia liked southwestern music by Native Americans) she asked for different animal hand puppets, (Julia liked animals) a poetry book, pen and notebook for writing, and possible bible stories - "short ones" she suggested.

We started the program Feb. 18, 2002.

The very next day I brought several animal puppets and Julia said: "Before we start, I want to name these little guys."

The green lady frog became Mumpack, the white fluffy sheep became "OK Goodlookin'" and the several mice became "Missy Mouse, White mouse, Mister Mouse, and Grey Mouse."

We started to make a little play for children, but Julia ran out of steam and asked me to read to her. She also asked for music. We chose a poetry book called The Prophet by Khahil Gibran and the music of a southwestern flautist. The poem we chose opened up real conversation on what Julia had experienced in her life, and how she had struggled.

Julia always wanted to write poetry and told me part of her heritage was native American. With some difficulty, she spoke about her life growing up, which included a much-abused childhood - sexual as well as physical - at an early age. She left home in her teens, and went onto the street and into prostitution, because, she said: "I had no education for anything else." Her life centered on the lives of other ladies of the night and she made friendships which, she said: "That's what kept me going. I became pregnant twice and decided to keep my babies." She smiled then and her face became tender. "Oh how I loved my babies!" she exclaimed. "I would also babysit other friends' babies so they could work the night and we would get together after they came home and talk about our dreams."

When she spoke about her life as a prostitute, she said something very interesting: "You know, people need to love each other and themselves more. I mean really love; I don't mean the sexual stuff. If they loved each other, and themselves, we prostitutes would be out of a job."

She was so proud of the fact that later she had become a barber. Apparently she had saved up enough money to put herself through barber school. "I was a pretty good barber too!" she exclaimed.

Julia and I decided to write some poetry. It was a day when she was weak and didn't want too much activity. We talked about ideas and this poem emerged:

I'd like to be a bird
and fly and fly and fly.
I'd like to be pretty too
and I'd be free.
I'd fly into mountains
because I like mountains.
I like them a lot because they're strong.
They stand throughout the ages
seeing generations rise and fall,
all the comings and goings
of this old world.
Maybe I'll be a sparrow,
a sweet little innocent bird.

During her stay at the home, Julia received cards and magazines, and we decided to take them out of her bedside table, cut out some pictures and tape them all over her room. She directed me as to where to put each picture and seemed as happy as I felt with the result.

It had been raining just before I arrived and we decided to write a poem about the rain. The poems she dictated told me a lot about her world inside:

RAIN

I wish it would rain more.
Rain makes plants grow.
The lilacs are more purple,
and the cucumbers grow greener,
because of the rain.

If there's no rain,
everything stops growing,
and life dries up.
You plant seeds and they
stop growing,
like people's hopes.

Rain is pretty.
The desert becomes alive.
the desert animals
slake their thirst.
They all need water
to drink.

I like to go playin' in the rain,
to get wet, feel the rain on my skin.
That's a good feeling.
I feel clean.

Rain is part of God's job
to give the world
water to drink
and to wash the world
clean again.

Will you give me another
drink of water?

As our time together increased Julia began to relax and seemed to be healing inside. We visited the chapel; Julia in her wheel chair, carrying my guitar. "Sing me a nice hymn!" she would command and I would sing hymns to her. Her cussing had stopped and she hadn't thrown anything at anybody for a quite awhile. One of the nurses commented to me that Julia was now "very peaceful." She added: "Honestly, she's so serene; it's getting boring around here!" Julia and I made a tapestry together, with bright colors, little people with happy faces, and a sun smiling down on everyone through the rain.

Before I left for Canada, I went back to see Julia. She rummaged through her bedside table and pulled out a well-loved teddy bear. "I've been saving this for you," she said, her big brown eyes sparkling. "I know I'm not going to be here much longer, and I want my teddy to have a good home."

Teddy came back to Canada with me and I've had Teddy for almost seven years. Little Ginny spotted him a few days ago and wanted to play with him, too. Somehow, I know Julia wouldn't mind, since she loved animals so much.

Apparently Julia died a peaceful death. She simply stopped breathing. As I think of her I'm grateful for all the many gifts she gave me by shyly sharing with me her thoughts and talents and telling me one of her valuable conclusions from her life. Whether any one of us is a queen or a lady of the night, are we not all of one Spirit inside? Is it simply a matter of one's life circumstances and life choices that sets us apart from each other? Sometimes a person has to make difficult choices to barely survive. Julia is God's child, just like we all are God's children.

I'm glad I met Julia and I know she is safe now in God's land of Spirit.

Thomas: (also known as Tom or Tommy): ━━━━━━━━━

We learn to do something by doing it. There is no other way - John Holt, educator.

Tom had been the head of an organization until he suffered a massive stroke. They thought he had died, but medical personnel managed to resuscitate him. I met Tom during the month of February. He was able to nod his head for "yes" and close his eyes for "no." He attempted to talk, opening his mouth and making sounds.

He tired easily and after several minutes he went to sleep. He seemed to enjoy being touched and I massaged his hands and his neck, re-positioned him, and gave passive exercises to his arms and legs.

His neighbor was listening to TV which was very loud. I asked him if he would mind turning it down during my visits with Tom and he was very agreeable and also amiable. I wondered if he would like to take part in some exercises which would increase the social aspect of Tom's life. In thinking of programs, the following came to mind.

1. Range of motion exercises to music. Tom prefers instrumentals and likes Kenny G.
2. Reading to Tom and using photos of his children and family.
3. Reminiscent therapy centering on his own accomplishments and how they related now to his family's accomplishments which reflect back to him.

Tom and I worked on his right hand and arm which initially was difficult for him since his hand had begun to contracture and his arm jerked involuntarily. We worked to music, (Kenny G) and as we worked I spoke to him about how working with his arm was also stimulating some parts of his brain. He looked at me intently and then Tom bent his head and wept.

As time progressed, so did Tommy, but very slowly. I'd say to him: "Come on Tommy, and let's repair some of the stroke damage in that brain of yours," as I lifted his arm and moved it around.

We continued working on his arms and legs which gradually began to loosen up. Tommy seemed to gather more control of both his arm and legs. Surprisingly, his left arm, which seemed to be completely paralyzed, began to move also, and with that Tom looked surprised and then began to smile.

Later, he showed interest in a book on painting which had the artist's written comments. As I read to him, he nodded "yes" several times and I knew then that although on the outside he was handicapped he was "definitely there" on the inside.

I learned again that it is so important to reach the person inside and not to become emotionally involved and reactive to the pathos which the person demonstrates and struggles with on the outside. All I know is that Tommy responded well because he thought I expected him to, and he was seeing the results, even though they were in baby steps. I think it's so important to keep that spark, or flame, going. It's called hope.

As the days and weeks progressed Tommy was able to touch his fingers to his nose, and even waggle his fingers at me to tease me. He had learned to "think relax" and then his body responded. One day I came to see him and he was not in his room. I returned three times but still no Tom. I finally caught up with him and kidded him about copping out on me. We talked about his grandchildren and his children, whom I had met, and Tommy smiled.

He had taken to leaving his room and enlarging his parameters and I felt he was on his way to moving ahead with the person he was inside. I noticed his hand strength was improving. Two of his grandchildren were now working with his hands, arms and legs and he was improving nicely. He had reconnected with his family who loved him dearly. There was hope again, for all of them that he was not lost to them. I do not know what happened to Tommy after I left, but I do know that the program we set up together made a big difference.

In many ways Tom has made a big difference in the lives of his children and grandchildren, before - when he was healthy - as well as after his stroke. He also made a big difference in my life.

In the summer of 2009 I too had a stroke. I could not do some things like I used to.

However, I thought of Tommy, and said to myself: "If Tommy did it, so can I!" and kept on trying. Instead of getting impatient, frustrated and giving up - which I started to do with myself initially - I still kept trying like Tom and I've made great strides. Although Tom has graduated to the next kingdom, he is still with me as an example of courage, strength and perseverance. I believe God created many ways to solve a problem and we simply have to latch onto a different way of doing things and get back some of our abilities. To create a miracle we must believe we can, and always maintain hope.

I'm sure hope was in the hearts of all the people Jesus Christ healed. They came to him in droves and he healed them all. Hope must be kept alive, at all costs, in order for a miracle to happen.

Cynthia: Never Underestimate Spirit: ━━━━━━━━━━

Life shrinks or expands in proportion to one's courage - Anais Nin- French Author

This next story is about another client whose name was Cynthia. I was told that she had her own set routine: visiting her dad, who was in another wing of the building, going out for walks and taking part in activities within the community.

Cynthia was born with cerebral palsy, which happened during her birth, when oxygen was cut off from her during the time her mother delivered her and this left part of her brain affected. She had definite ideas and did not wish to deviate from the routine she had set up for herself. I certainly respected that. The staff gave her to me since they noticed her energy level was diminishing. They also mentioned she was recovering from an operation to remove both her breasts which had become cancerous.

When we first met, I had tracked Cynthia down to her dad's room and made arrangements to meet with her in her room at 10 a.m. We discussed her likes and dislikes and scheduling and agreed to meet on Wednesday mornings at the same time.

Cynthia was about 5ft6inches, with blondish hair, still a bit curly from a permanent last year. Her eyes were a faded blue in an oval shaped face. She wore no make-up. When she walked, her toes pointed slightly in towards each other. Her shoulders slumped a bit even when she stood or sat, which made her back look slightly humped.

She told me she knew how to read, but needed large print. As time went on, she opened up about her life and I learned that she had been in a special class for handicapped children in elementary school, but in high school she managed to keep up with the students in the regular classes.

"Boy was that ever a revelation!" she told me. "You know, many of those normal kids were much less motivated than I was!" Then, with great pride, she told me she had made the honor lists both in junior and senior high school.

She continued her life story: "After high school, they sent me to a Baptist Bible College because I loved the bible so much. That was a real shocker! The students all knew their bible verses, but to apply them was another matter." She took a breath and continued: "I found that some of them could even twist any situation around and be justified as to what they were trying to do, or get away with, by quoting a bible verse." She told me that after two years she finished there, and was relieved to return to her Roman Catholic Church.

She said, "It felt like I was coming home."

Cynthia continued to tell me about her life, and how she fell in love with a fellow she met when she was attending the special school for handicapped children.

She said she longs to see him again. They had planned to get married and have kids, but Cynthia told me: "I sure am glad now we didn't. I can't take care of anyone but me and yet I wanted six children. That shows you how much I knew about biology!"

As she was relating her story, I asked how she felt about her recent operation to remove her breasts. She hung her head. "My body is so scarred and I hate to have to look at myself."

We talked about the many women who have had the same operation, with the same scars and she was able to re-frame those scars into being the scars of battle, and that she and many others were the warriors and survivors of the huge battle against cancer. This seemed to give Cynthia more confidence in herself, and she began to walk up straight instead of humping her shoulders. She often spoke of the sweetheart relationship she had enjoyed when in elementary school. "I sure would like to see my sweetheart again," she kept repeating.

That gave me an idea. I asked her if she had ever considered learning how to use a computer. She said no, but that she'd like to learn. In addition, we planned a program initially to get her started on activities in the home, and it included the following:

1. Sing hymns in the chapel.
2. See what puppets are all about.
3. Read and maybe write some poetry.

I saw Cynthia each day for awhile, and also made a special request to our administrator to find out if there was anyone within the facility who could teach Cynthia to use a computer. There was.

It took some time to get the computer project off the ground. In the meantime, Cynthia and I sang hymns in the chapel and began working with the hand puppets. She liked the dragon, calling him a "friendly dragon."

She was interested in the book about puppetry, and told me: "Oh, my goodness, this is a lot more work that I thought it would be." When we read poetry she said she would like to write one of her own. She dictated and I wrote it down. Here it is.

Inside me there is only one day at a time.
Be a person who is happy and free.
Be the person who loves openly.
Be the person the world likes to know.
Be the person who helps people grow.

I do not know whether Cynthia got her computer, or whether she was able to make a contact with her sweetheart who had moved away to another state

Although Cynthia has passed through the veil into the next kingdom, I hope she did learn the computer and find her true love before she died. She deserved to, since she had perseverance, dignity and looked at life through a very clear window.

I cherish the three people I have written about. I value what they taught me. For Julia, and Thomas, who became prisoners in their own bodies because of their afflictions, John Milton wrote a poem long ago which included the line: "They also serve, who only stand and wait." For Cynthia I loved her truth. She adjusted to her situation and made the best of it.

Leo Rosten wrote a poem which reminds me of my three clients, who met their changed lives first with grief and then acceptance, and who grew beyond their anguish to find new meanings. They found out that they "mattered" very much to all of us.

In some way, however small and secret, each of us is a little mad....

Everyone is lonely at bottom and cries to be understood; but we can never entirely understand someone else, and each of us remains part stranger even to those who love us . . . It is the weak who are cruel; gentleness is to be expected only from the strong . . . . Those who do not know fear are not really brave, for courage is the capacity to confront what can be imagined . . . . You can understand people if you look at them - no matter how old or impressive they are - as if they are children. For most of us never mature; we simply grow taller . . . . Happiness comes only when we push our brains and hearts to the farthest reaches of which we are capable . . . . The purpose of life is to MATTER; to count, to stand for something, to have it make some difference that we lived at all." Leo Rosten

(Leo Rosten was an American teacher, academic and humorist. He lived from April 11, 1908, to Feb 19, 1997. I particularly like this poem and keep it in my room to refer to often.)

CHAPTER **18**

The Spirit of Murphy

We are all 'Warriors of Light' when we come here . A Warrior knows that the ends do not justify the means. Because there are no ends, there are only means. Life carries him from unknown to unknown. Each moment is filled with this mystery: The Warrior does not know where he came from nor where he is going. - Paul Coelho, Warrior of the Light.

My friend, Sharon, who sold real estate in the Desert Pueblo Mobile Home Park in Tucson, Arizona, was despondent. "I don't know how I'll be able to sell that one," she said, referring to one of her client's homes. "It's so dark and needs a lot of work. But it is a good solid home if someone wanted to fix it up."

My husband, Ray, and I were curious so she took us to see the home. We both liked the layout and the owner was desperate to sell. Ray and I whispered between ourselves: "Why don't we make an offer, and if it goes, we can fix it up and sell it"

We made the offer and it was accepted. We were on!

First, we cleaned the place, stripping away the old stained rugs, tossing out the previous owner's golf trophies which had been left behind and clearing out most of the old broken-down furniture.

Ray began to paint and I began to clean. It took 27 gallons of paint to brighten both the inside and the outside of the mobile, but it was beginning to sparkle.

I got to know the next-door neighbor, Yvonne, who gave me a bit of a history about the people who had lived there before. Apparently the husband looked like Col. Sanders with white beard, mustache and paunch belly. The residents in Desert Pueblo Park called him "Doc" because he had been connected in some way to the medical profession at one time.

Doc, who Yvonne said had a good sense of humor but occasionally a short fuse, had suffered from blindness and was prone to wandering the house in the dark well after midnight doing odd jobs. His wife, Peggy, was a well-loved woman who was described as friendly and warm. They were both in their 90s and very sound in mind. They were applauded for their dancing abilities at the monthly dances held in our park club house.

Apparently Doc had suffered either a massive heart attack or stroke and had been taken by ambulance to the hospital where he died. Peggy had gone to a nursing home shortly after Doc's death and the house had been vacant for some time.

We were up to our elbows in paint and renovations when my daughter, Laura, arrived from Victoria, B.C., Canada, for a visit. I had cleaned up the room where Doc had slept. I hadn't had time to buy a new bed, but cleaned up the one that was in the room, put on new mattress covers and clean sheets for her, and hoped she'd manage until we shopped for a new bed. I was worried that Laura would be cold because the room itself never seemed to warm up. Sometimes it was icy cold in there.

After the first night, Laura looked a little tired, but I thought she was probably just adjusting after the plane trip. However, she complained that the people next door must have been having a late-night party, since she heard voices late into the night. That was strange, because the man next door always went to bed early. The second night she said it was just as bad, so she had put her radio on with the earphones. But even that didn't help, because her little radio had crackled loudly, and she couldn't even hear the music.

Laura looked terrible that morning and after the third night she was distraught. We both were. We had both been awakened very early hearing a painful agonized groan. I was more than suspicious as to what was going on and we discussed it. Laura was scheduled to make a short trip up to Salt Lake City to see her brother, George, and we saw her off at the airport.

As soon as I returned to the house, I went next door and talked to Yvonne. I asked her specific questions about the previous tenants and what she told me confirmed my suspicions. Returning to Doc's room, I painted it again, cleaned the bathroom thoroughly again and tossed out the bed and bookcases. I went shopping for new furniture, some pictures for the walls, new curtains, a lamp and side table and a scatter rug for the floor. When the room was complete, I had a shower, put on clean clothes, read my Bible, said a prayer for help, and then re-entered Doc's room. I brought my classical guitar in with me and laid it on the new bed beside me as I sat down.

Then, I said aloud: "All right, Doc, I know you're here and I want to talk to you. I need to know why you are still here."

My head nearly burst with the tremendous outpouring of anger, frustration and outrage which was heaped upon me.

"How could you and your husband have the nerve to come into my house and start ripping up the rugs, making renovations which I haven't ordered?" Doc asked. "What gave you the right to throw away my golf trophies? And where the heck was Peggy - or Margaret to you - because I've been waiting for her to come home? And who was that young woman sleeping in my bed for the past two nights?"

Wow! I had been right in my suspicions.

Although my heart was beating faster than usual, I took a deep breath and said: "Your name is Murphy and they call you Doc. I know that because Yvonne told me. We bought your house from your wife, Peggy. The night, quite awhile ago now, when you went to the hospital, you died. Your spirit must have come straight back here to wait for Peggy. But she is in a nursing home now. The house now belongs to us."

I told Doc we hadn't had time to change the name on the front of the home, but we'd do it right away.

"We didn't want your golf trophies," I continued, "because they don't mean anything to us. I'm sorry if your feelings are hurt about that. I didn't know that you were here at first, although I was aware that there was something angry here.

"When you started bothering my daughter, I realized it was you, and you were still here. I know you didn't mean to hurt her either."

There was a silence for awhile. I continued: "I think you may have some people with you who have been trying to get you to move along with them. They are your guardian angels and mean only the utmost good for you. You will be much happier where you are going and there might even be someplace you can play golf there. This is no longer your home."

I sang a hymn for Doc called the Benediction. This is a beautiful hymn sung usually at the end of a meeting asking for blessings before going on. I sang to him a selection of other hymns and songs which I loved.

As I sang, I felt him relaxing and the anger dispersing.

I spoke to him again: "Doc, I'd like you to go with your angels and I know you will be much happier, for you will receive more information about Peggy and also meet all your relatives and friends."

Saying a prayer for him aloud, I sat on the new bed for a while and then left the room, but kept the door open.

Laura came back a few days later and was delighted with the bright, fresh cheerfulness in the room. She also slept well and enjoyed the last few days of her stay.

I have come across one of Laura's writings and include some parts of it here as it is her own perspective and experience which sheds light on this situation from a different view point.

Laura wrote:

"I should first mention that I have been consistently pursuing my own personal relationships with my Spirit Guides for some time. My ability to sense them and even converse with them by means of thought connection has improved considerably over the past year or so.

"Well, on that first night when I was awakened and was feeling disturbed and perplexed, I put on my (music) and settled back into a comfortable meditation. I received a signal that my Spirit Guides or family spirits were close at hand. This certainly made me feel less fearful and more comfortable and I was able to settle down and eventually fall asleep.

"The next night was similar. I had taken a sleeping pill, but was awakened at the same time, about 2:30 in the morning. I arose once again to read and eventually put on my meditation disc which allowed me to go to sleep after some time.

"The third night, however, was an entirely different story. I took a sleeping pill and went to bed quite a bit later after mamma and Ray had settled into "snoozeville." While deep within slumber, I heard an excruciating groan of agony and was awakened into an abrupt alert state. I again heard the groan and became quite agitated as I again experienced this strange sensation of being observed and of 'being in the way.'

"The feeling of this strange heaviness was more intense this night and when I looked at the clock, it was again 2:30 a.m. I tried to read but was unable to focus. When I put my Discman on to meditate, there was a strong sense of interference which made it impossible to hear the voice and I could not meditate as I had wished.

"I eventually lay quietly until I slipped into a slumber state and then found myself in a clear, bright dream. In my dream, I arose out of bed and went down the hall to mamma's and Ray's room.

"I was greeted at the door by mamma and she was wearing a long dark ruana (a poncho-like garment worn as a wrap). It was my intention to tell mama of the strange energy which existed in my room and inform her that the energy, which appeared to be masculine, had been there for the last three days. I was, however, unable to communicate with her, as my ability to speak had completely dissolved.

"This was frustrating as well as overwhelming to me, and, at the same time, frightening to know that I was unable to speak. I realized that there was a physical force that was holding me against the wall that prevented me from getting any closer to my mom. I became even more overwhelmed and experienced myself literally 'checking out' or in other words becoming unconscious. My body began to fall and my mother reached out and scooped me into her arms, wrapping me in her ruana. She then looked upwards and began to slowly ascend upwards like she was ready to begin to fly. I then awoke.

"The reason I awoke was because I again heard that awful groan that was full of anguish. This time, however, I heard my mom rise from her bed and knew she had heard the sound as well. I met her outside my room and began babbling about this strange and disturbing energy within my room. Mamma concurred that she had also heard the strange sound, and led me to the couch in the front room to more closely listen to my frantic description of the past three days.

"Mamma believed my description which was a relief to me, as I was quite out of my familiar realm by this time.

"When I returned (from Salt Lake City), I was quite apprehensive about returning to my room. At the airport mamma told me that she did, in fact, connect with spirit whose name was Doc, in his room, and had an in-depth conversation with him. It is my hope that my mother will at some time include her experiences in writing, so that I can add her part to my journal.

"That night was silent for me. I slept through the entire night soundly. I realize how valuable this experience has been for me. Not only was it an indication to me of my own emerging psychic sensitivities, but it was a lesson for me as to where I needed to develop. My mother was a wonderful and compassionate mentor for me. She dealt with the situation with courage and understanding, not to mention with caring and love."

A few days after Laura had left for home, I was standing in the living room when something directed me to the old bookcase which was the last remnant of Doc's furniture. A black three-ring binder was lying on a shelf there. It contained all the warranties for the appliances, something I already knew as I had leafed quickly through it previously.

However, something (a Spirit?) told me to read the back pages. They were yellow, very thin, faded, and old and the type seemed very faint, but legible.

I discovered that Doc had been a medical equipment technician, part of a medical team headed by Dr. Arthur D. Cruz and Dr. Robert L. Price. This team of medical equipment technicians had been sent to Nigeria after the former Nigerian civil war in Africa, (July 6, 1967 to Jan.15, 1970).

As I accessed information about the Nigerian war from the Internet, I learned about the problems which precipitated the conflict. I began to understand the immense problems the medical equipment team had faced as they tried to pursue the goals set out for them. Here's a little background I gleaned from the internet.

Around 1905, Great Britain had taken over a large swath of West Africa and called it Nigeria. The British political ideology divided Nigeria into three regions, North, West and East. This exacerbated the already well-developed economic, political and social competition among Nigeria's very different ethnic groups.

The prominent ethnic group in the northern region of Nigeria was called the Hausa-Frelane, and was much larger in numbers than the west and east. In the eastern part were the Igbo, and in the western part were the Yoruba. The Hausa-Frelane and the Yoruba had similar political systems with a form of government which involved a powerful Sultan for the Hausa peoples, and Emirs and an all powerful Oba for the Yoruba. They both followed an Islamic tradition. Political decisions in these two groups were to be obeyed without question.

The eastern Igbo people lived mostly in democratically organized autonomous communities. Decisions among the Igbo's were made by a general assembly in which every man could participate.

In the north, Britain found it convenient to rule indirectly through the Emirs and the Sultan. This perpetuated the indigenous political system of authority. The result was that the area remained closed to Western Education and influences. Christian missionaries were excluded.

The rich eastern Igbo's sent their sons to British universities, while the south west's Emirs maintained traditional and religious institutions. This limited social change. As a result in 1960 at the time of independence, the northern part was the most underdeveloped area in Nigeria with a literacy rate of two per cent compared to more than nine per cent in the west. The south eastern Igbo peoples enjoyed a much higher literacy level since they had contact with western education in addition to the primary education program of the pre-independence south eastern regional government. In the 1940s and 1950s, the Igbo and Yoruba parties were fighting for independence from Britain.

Basically, the Nigerian-Biafran civil war was a political conflict caused by the attempted succession of the eastern Igbo province of Nigeria as the self-proclaimed Republic of Biafra.

The team was to locate and establish all the medical diagnostic equipment which the United States, Canada and Britain had given to Nigeria, at the end of the war.

This equipment had been sent to the various Nigerian Disaster Centers, but the different types of equipment had never arrived to their destinations. It included X-ray machines, and other new and very expensive medical equipment.

Apparently, there had been many difficulties to overcome, communication and red tape being some of them. The team had to unravel the problem areas in order to accomplish their mission. Doc Murphy was, in fact, named Francis Murphy and was a well-respected medical equipment technician. He was sent over with another technician, Al Goss, and they were to establish the remaining equipment in the hospitals of Nigeria in March, 1970. As I read through some of "Doc's" reports there was definitely a sense of frustration at times. Although I was tempted to include "Doc's" reports in this book, I will not do so, because they are copies of government reports. I will not jeopardize his memory in any way. My respect for Francis "Doc" Murphy is great. I can say that some of the equipment was found in barns and warehouses, and were trucked out and established by "Doc" and Al in their proper destined places.

Mr. Goss and Francis "Doc" Murphy were highly commended getting the much-needed medical equipment to different disaster hospitals in Nigeria. They accomplished their mission with honor and were highly commended by Drs. Cruz and Price who headed the mission.

I am grateful Doc came back to direct me to those faded yellow pages at the back of the black three-ringed binder. Although I have never met him in life, it was a pleasure to meet him in the afterlife, before he went on.

CHAPTER 19

The Tucson Writer's group and the Over Pass Café

We are all one, and are here to help each other - DorisMae Honer

Joyce and I talked one day about forming a writing group. She belonged to one, which had decided to have no further members.

So Joyce started a new writing group with herself, Julie, Virginia, Jeanne, Fran and I as members. We meet each Monday morning at 9 a.m. and take turns reading what we have written. The group listens and makes comments.

Fran wrote a wonderful poem on being a flamenco dancer. Virginia described the many facets of her life, from construction to a passion for history. Julie and I share a deep love of music. Jeanne came later and has contributed greatly to our writing group.

I want to include a poem I wrote thanking the ladies and later an experience that Joyce wrote about.

I think our life experiences are rich and valuable. Isn't it imperative that they be recorded in some way for the people who come after us? There are lessons in each experience which are pure gold.

To the Writers Group Jan 16, 2008:

On Being Thankful ──────────────────

I've travelled quite a bit,
on my life's journey,
seen most of Canada, and the USA,
been to some countries in South America
and a few in Europe.
The best part of it all is
meeting the world's peoples,
all of them "just good folks."
For these many blessings, I am thankful.
I've been considered rich, by some people,
and I've also been dirt poor.
It was when I was completely broke and alone,
that I learned the most.
My thirty year marriage
had dissolved into divorce,
and in the time I was really needy,
I was given kindness and caring
far beyond my expectations.
I have so much to be thankful for.

Thank you once again,
Shirley, of the Salvation Army,
for taking the last two dollars I had
and giving me six nurse's uniforms,
a pair of white pantyhose and
a new pair of nurse's shoes,
all in my size.
You were as excited as I was
about my new job,
and my brand new life.
Thanks to you Margaret Orr,

the Chronic Care Facility Director,
for becoming my friend,
as well as my employer.
You listened to my anguish
even when I wasn't talking.
You were just THERE.
and treated me as your equal.

Thank you, my loving sister Margaret,
for knowing and telling me that
"This too will pass".
Thank you for believing in me,
even when all I could do
was put one foot in front of the other
and hope for the best.

Thank you God, for putting all those
many kindly people on my path, all of them
nurturers in their own way.
Thank you for listening to my raging questions
and quelling them quickly
with your "one liner" sense of humor.

Thank you to Sharon, for being my friend
through the good times and the sad ones,
and for having such a beautiful and loving spirit.
Thank you Ray, my solid guardian of love.
I was so sick with shingles that
I simply wanted to just pass on, and almost did.
You took good care of me so I wouldn't.
You love me even when sometimes you
can't understand parts of the "me" I am.
Thank you for believing in US.

Thank you Joyce, for knowing the value
of each human experience, and asking us
to share, through the medium of writing.
Thank you Fran, the Flamenco dancer,
Virginia, the historian, and builder,
Julie, my fellow music lover,
and Jeanne, a shining soul.

Thank you all for the journey
we are about to take together
into our inner worlds
where God lives.

One morning at the writer's group, we were discussing graffiti and murals on walls. I happened to mention that Ray and I sometimes go to the Overpass Café in Tucson, Ariz., for breakfast and the walls there are covered with paintings of the Arizona desert, mountains, horses, cattle, a truck and a woman named Jodie on her front porch.

I had met the artist when he was in the midst of painting and he had remarked that he had never had a lesson; he was just a cowboy who loved to draw and paint. His name was John Gibbons, a slight man who looked like and dressed like a ranch hand. He didn't talk much when I knew him but answered my questions as he painted. He used the walls as his canvas.

The members in the writer's group were fascinated and I told them all about Jodie, too. Jodie had been a waitress in the café. She is always pleasant, quick and efficient. When the café's owner wanted to retire, Jodie bought the business. It was Jodie who hired John Gibbons to paint the wonderful murals on the walls.

The writer's club wanted to see the murals and meet Jodie. We met at Joyce's at 8 a.m. and formed a car caravan to the Overpass Café. It was really crowded when we arrived, but Jodie had reserved the back booth which accommodates at least eight people. The writer's group was all eyes, not only for the murals but also for the people.

One of our members was using a walker and it was difficult for her to get to the reserved area until a man jumped up and moved chairs for her so that she could pass. He must have been a hard-working laborer, as were his buddies. His face was deeply lined and tanned, as were his muscular arms and his scarred, large-boned hands.

Jodie and her husband work hard in the Over Pass; she takes orders and he cooks, although Jodie often will do the cooking and serving herself.

She is one of the hardest working people I have ever met. She remembers how people like their eggs, toast and coffee; each and every one of us. The first year I went, I was amazed. Then in returning after being away six months, she still remembered. How, I don't know.

Jodie's a very colorful part of the real Tucson spirit and personifies this in her Over Pass Cafe. She has a great appreciation of art which shows in her featuring the murals of John Gibbons on the walls of her cafe. The writer's group was entranced with the artistry.

I'm including a few writings from the group; I know you will enjoy them. In both writings you will find the essence of Spirit.

Joyce was a kindergarten teacher, retired now, is very sensitive to people's emotions, has a wonderful sense of humor, loves music and plays a mean piano, and is a kind and spiritual person. She has the warm friendly appearance that makes people comfortable and happy. She is easy to talk to and fun to be with. I love her writings.

Then He Was Gone - Joyce Hodges, 2008.

I never took care of the car. Bob always filled it with gas and kept track of all the maintenance for me. He died of meningitis one weekend, leaving me totally off guard. My son offered to have his father-in-law fill in for Bob on all the automobile functions. I found the suggestion kind, but totally absurd. I could do this on my own, I thought to myself.

The following day, I was almost out of gas and drove to the

nearest gas station. It was bitter outside with a cold November wind blowing debris all over the ground. As I opened the door, a blast of air went up my jacket. I fooled with the gas cap, but it wouldn't budge. I remember thinking that I never appreciated Bob doing all these "taken-for-granted" jobs.

Off came one glove. Maybe the cap needed a human touch. Still, it wouldn't co-operate. Looking up, I noticed a man who would have fit nicely into a Santa Claus suit. His appearance made me think of a "Hells Angels" member in good standing. However, I preferred the Santa image.

Marching over, I looked at him and related my tale of woe. Trailing after me, he took his powerful hand and wrapped it around the cap. In one turn he had it off. He turned his head ever so slightly and said in a soft voice: "Perhaps you should let your husband take care of this." My voice quivering, I told him my husband had died a week earlier.

He turned away and then back: "Why don't you let me check your oil and windshield wipers?" My head nodded and I thanked him for helping me. He went back to his truck and I paid for the gas.

As I was climbing back into the car, I felt a touch on my shoulder. I looked up at my Santa who was patting me on the arm. Out of his mouth came such a kind remark. This big tough guy in almost a whisper spoke these words that I've never forgotten: "You're going to be okay. I know you're going to be okay." Then he was gone.

Fran is a tall slim classy lady from New York, and has written poetry all her life. Fran speaks with a New Yorker accent, and has been a "city girl" all her life. She injects humor, as well as wisdom into her poems and some of them ride like the wind.

"The Flamenco Dancer" is exciting whimsical and brilliantly enjoyable. Fran wrote A Solitary Soul shortly after her husband passed away. This poem points out how important the world of silence is in the healing process, where one can communicate with one's Spirit.

The Flamenco Dancer - Francine Atkins, June 1997. ━━━

A wise old man once asked me,
"If you couldn't be you, who would you be?
Now think before you answer."
I didn't have to think a lot,
I knew right there, on that very spot.
I would be a Flamenco dancer!

I'd be born in a cave somewhere in Spain,
and I'd barely know how to write my name,
but I would be a Flamenco dancer.
My hair pitch black as the midnight sky
my feet so fast I could almost fly,
I would wear a rose behind my ear.

The crowd would clap and
they would cheer for me,
the wondrous Flamenco dancer.
Castanets would click at a furious pace
and I'd see joy on every face.
I'd wear a gown as bright as flame
with polka dots and ruffled train.

I'd be a Flamenco dancer.
Perhaps someday in another life
I won't be a mother, I won't be a wife
I'll be a gypsy born in Spain
and everyone will speak the name
of the wondrous Flamenco dancer!

A Solitary Soul - Francine Atkins, 2009 ━━━━━━━━

There are times it seems to me
it's very lovely just to be
a solitary Soul.
To snuggle in a cozy chair
with peaceful silence everywhere,
a Solitary Soul.
Hear the birds how sweet their song!
They've been here all along,
but you can't hear them through the clatter,
laughter, coughing, chatter, chatter.
These are the times you need to be
A Solitary Soul.

CHAPTER **20**

The Victoria Writer's Group

We meet every Wednesday after yoga, at 11 o'clock. There are five of us, Agnes and Gordon Craig, Carmen Comrie, Shirley Bassett and me. Our writings are about our life's experiences, and we discuss the writings and give feedback regarding the style, whenever it occurs to us. The group is warm, very caring, and always full of surprises. The writing group which was started at Gordon United Church in Langford, British Columbia has a distinct character of its own. In previous chapters I included writings by Shirley Barrett. Now I include another writing by Gordon Craig.

Gordon Craig is a retired minister, a large man with a long grey beard, a kind and slightly raspy voice, and a very observant eye. He is a real "thinker" and goes after details like a British bull dog on the hunt. His story demonstrates the power which Spirit influenced on him, and which changed his life.

Searing Memories: by Gordon M. Craig. ━━━━━━━━

A question many of us are asked as we get older is what are your most vivid memories? What from your childhood and youth are "seared" into your consciousness? The problem is I was asked about the ones that happened within my family; the hurts and emotional scars that are raised by family abuse of one sort or another. Yes, there was more abuse of one sort or another in my family than any of us kids care to remember. However, most of it was the garden variety. One example I clearly remember which eroded my inner self like the Chinese water torture method. An example is, when you're told constantly that you'll never amount to anything, that you're a nobody because you can't add up the calendar numbers like dad could, it clearly had a tremendous effect on a growing boy. I got to thinking then if I was junk, then so be it.

But a little black boy said, quite ungrammatically, "God don't make no junk!" Indeed! And I agree with that! He sure don't!

There was one small incident, which became an absolute turning point in my life. It happened to me in a very ordinary worship service at Asbury and West United Church in west Toronto. Right off the bat, too. The call to worship was, "Now then, you are ambassadors for Christ. God is making his appeal through you. Be reconciled to God". This emphasis on the second person was startling to me. I had always taken the bible teachings as more or less universal, with no particular person addressed except perhaps individuals in the bible, like Isaiah in the temple, or Moses at the burning bush. Wrong! Whoever Paul was talking to in 2 Corinthians didn't matter to me---at that searing moment he was talking to ME!!

At that time I was in first year college, with vague ideas of ministry and service. Nothing particular had taken root in my psyche. This call to worship struck me right between the eyes. "You Gordon, are my messenger." Here was a straight order, not just some general request. I responded as Moses and Isaiah, not to mention lots of others with a "Who, Me?" response.

At that point I knew this was serious stuff, not just some "religious experience" but something that was to change my life forever. I was no longer the mousy nerd Gordon. I was to be one of God's ambassadors to the world. I was soon to be known as Reverend Gordon Craig!

What happened over the next six or seven years was a whirl, essentially coming out of that experience. First present myself to the session of my home church, WoodGreen United in Toronto East

Presbytery. Then work hard at my studies (something I had not been doing, admittedly, over the last year or so) then on to Emmanuel College for my theological training, and eventually to Danforth Ave. United Church (now Eastminister United) for the truly searing part: the laying on of hands, to ordain me to Christ's ministry. This experience was particularly memorable to me because my minister and mentor Rev. Ray McLeary was part of the ceremony.

The following years are rich with meeting and helping so many fine people in northern communities of Ontario, and southern Quebec. Not only did I learn to understand and helped, as well as be helped by people in totally new sub cultures, but I also discovered I had a real affinity to learning new languages. My experiences were precious; I was living a life I never had dreamed possible for me. I received prayers and good sermons from all sorts of United and other churches. Who knows where I would be if it were not for the love and faith given to me by our sublime Father.

CHAPTER 21

The Spirit of Dis-ease

Your body is . . . the expression of your existence. So many of us are not in our bodies; really at home and vibrantly present there. Nor are we in touch with the basic rhythms that constitute our bodily life. We live outside ourselves—in our heads, our memories, and our longings -absentee landlords of our own estate - Gabrielle Roth- author, musician, music director.

According to "Answers.com" in the Internet the word ease means: a condition of being comfortable or relieved. It means freedom from pain, worry, or agitation, difficulty, hardship or effort.

From the same source the word dis-ease means a pathological condition of a part, organ, or system of an organism resulting from various causes, such as infection, genetic defect, or environment stress, and characterized by an identifiable group of signs or symptoms. The word dis-ease was used in middle English and originated from the Old French spelling des-aise, translated into English becoming dis-ease.

From the Internet, I was also given this explanation. The term "dis-ease" is used as a substitute for the word disease by individuals in healing communities who are aligned with wellness. In doing this it is their intent to place emphasis on the natural state of "ease" being imbalanced or disrupted, desiring not to give too much focus to a particular ailment.

I like to use the word dis-ease rather than the word disease for two reasons. Firstly a person diagnosed with the pathological condition often thinks of themselves as diseased, and therefore manifests disease. As time goes on they often become the disease relinquishing personality for disease symptoms. Secondly by using the word dis-ease, in my mind at least, it means one can regain one's ease, and should take every measure to become the person of ease and keep their personality and character.

A good example of this idea is that a particular person who has been diagnosed with diabetes would not say "I am a diabetic" but rather "I am challenged with diabetes."

Please don't give your personal power over to a language or a dis-ease! More and more people are discovering how the words we utter and write carry power and are altering our voices accordingly.

This chapter is very personal and I write it only because I believe many people have gone through the same various emotions which illness brings. I am hoping others who may have been consumed with fear over illness can take that "illness bull" by the horns and turn their own lives around. I use the word dis-ease rather than disease, since I believe it helps a person to fight, rather than stand and allow illness to take them over.

This then is my story of dis-ease.

A Poem on Being Sick ━━━━━━━━━━━━━━━━━━━━

Sometimes an illness can play hide and seek.
I was feeling like ME again,
and now I'm back to feeling
less than me.
Tomorrow I go back to see my doctor
because he called me and said,
"Come in Monday morning
At 10:45."

Is that to tell me that
all the blood samples
were normal? Or to
tell me they weren't?

I hope my inner alarm system
is wrong.
I hope that tomorrow
all my health will come back,
and all my energy too.

Next week I will have completed
seventy four years
of living on this earth.
If I made it this far,
Maybe I'll make it to
One hundred.
Who knows?
God knows - DorisMae Honer, October, 2008

The shock was upon me and I could not think clearly. My family doctor said I would soon need dialysis; that my kidney function was failing. Dialysis, I thought. How could this be happening to me? I had always been healthy, exercised regularly, was careful what I ate - or so I thought at the time.

My brain seemed to be clogged and I needed time to assimilate this terrible news. My doctor said he had arranged for me to be cared for by Dr. Gaylene Hargrave, a nephrology specialist.

"This cannot be," I told myself. "Out of the blue I am told my plans for the future were to be put on hold. Why had I not been told that my kidneys were failing long before this?"

I knew enough about medicine to know this simply does not happen overnight. Yes, I had been gradually feeling less energetic, but I attributed this to my advancing years.

My family doctor continued to tell me about Dr. Hargrave, but

I could not hear all he was saying because my thoughts were in a whizzing blur.

"No! No! This is impossible," I thought. "They must have mixed the lab reports with someone else's. I cannot believe that this is happening to me!"

I left the doctor's office with my husband Ray holding my hand and we were both silent.

We drove home and he tried to reassure me. I sat in a daze, not hearing anything he said.

The visit with Dr. Gaylene Hargrave was a little more informative. (Probably I could take in more information because I was now absorbing some of the brutal facts.) Dr. Hargrave is a tall, beautiful, carefully groomed woman, fashionably classic in her dress and appearance. Her voice is soft and reassuring and her beautiful smile brings a person confidence.

I gave permission for her to go ahead and order a kidney biopsy and felt like a limp wooden doll puppet, a marionette with strings attached to my arms, neck, head and back. I was going through the motions while someone unseen seemed to be re-designing my life, pulling the strings, planning my future and telling me the brutal facts.

My mind still seemed couched in absorbent cotton balls. My husband, Ray, must also have still been in shock. We were both silent on the drive home. I became aware that there was weeping and pain inside my head. Someone, or many "someones," was weeping in deep agony and grief.

The internal soul realization and impending loss began to creep into my heart. I heard the lamentation and felt the pain of all those folks who live in my inner world; who make up the person I am.

"No!" I said to myself. "I will not allow this to happen to me. I will fight this." I began to research the Internet for all I could learn about kidneys and kidney disease. I began to change my diet. But I still began to lose ground. I thought I had the flu; I began to lose weight quickly and lose the color in my cheeks and the energy to even get out of bed in the morning. Meanwhile, my family doctor went on vacation.

My health deteriorated further. I was having symptoms of a stomach ulcer. Later, I experienced terrible pain around my heart. Ray took me to the Victoria General Hospital's emergency for that and I was strapped to a monitor for six hours. An EKG was taken twice and also many samples of blood. The pain persisted. They gave me oral pain medication which didn't help. Then they gave me an injection which completely knocked out my memory. Thank heavens my husband was with me. The heart-monitor results were that the heart was in normal sinus rhythm.

When they discharged me, I did what I never thought I would do - I consulted a naturopathic practitioner, Dr. Kyle Morrison. He was referred to me by my acupuncturist, Dr. Stefen Rabnett.

Dr. Morrison interviewed me and then gave me an assignment to fill out my meal intake for a week. By this time I was so nauseated I couldn't eat much and my energy was so low I could hardly attend to any activities of daily living. I felt, and apparently looked, terrible.

During that first interview, and after intensive questioning, Dr. Morrison suggested I might have an allergy to wheat. In the second interview, he asked me more questions, taking notes in his book. He gave me a two-week diet to follow which was gluten free, as well as dairy and preservative free.

As I followed the diet I began to feel better. I had begun to have a weight problem after I got married and fought with it all my life. Now, I was losing weight even with the gluten-free diet, but this time it was nice and easy, like it should be.

My doctor returned from vacation and I sent a lab sample to be tested. On top of all the other problems, I had all the symptoms of a bleeding ulcer.

I learned from my acupuncture and naturopathic doctors that they consider healing to come from within and that healing has a definite mind/body/spirit connection. They encouraged positive outlooks; to be objective about anything negative and to drop it in favor of the positive thoughts which help the body to heal. I learned how important it is to give the body healthy nutrition, without preservatives and what is termed "junk food."

With the two-week gluten free, preservative free diet that Dr. Morrison gave me, I began to pick up energy and to feel much better. The pains around my heart and in my stomach disappeared. I was able to cook, clean, read books and was generally much more pleasant to be around.

The appointment for the renal clinic came and the first session was with Chris, the renal dietician. She was informative, encouraging and agreed almost completely with the diet that Dr. Morrison had given me.

The afternoon session consisted of four patients, a social worker, a nurse and the head of the renal clinic. The patients included a Chinese man accompanied by his son and his wife. There was also a middle-aged lady who said little, an elderly man from East India who, although he spoke English, did so with such a heavy accent that I had difficulty understanding him. He said he had brought his estimated kidney function rate up from 20 to 26 percent by using Hath Yoga. I mentioned that I had brought mine up from 15 to 23 percent.

It seemed to me that the nurse shot us both down, saying that nothing we did would help increase the kidney function. Maybe I didn't hear her correctly but that is what I understood her to say. The surprise and shock of that statement hit me very hard. The rest of the meeting was informative, but I left feeling angry and in despair regarding the "fact" that apparently my kidneys were doomed. In looking back on that first clinic, I am very grateful to that nurse. Her presentation made me so angry, that I was determined to fight all the odds and overcome this horrible situation.

As I processed all the information my anger turned into resolution. If I had understood the nurse correctly, and if the nurse knew what she was talking about, I could still preserve the kidney function I still have, and anyway, I believe in miracles, so I would work towards increasing my kidney function despite her initial statement. When I checked with Dr. Hargrave, she said that one must never give up, and miracles certainly do happen.

The renal clinic nurse did give us very valuable information, and I appreciate that she did her best. However, I have been doing everything in my own power to keep myself going and remain as healthy as I can possibly be. I am keeping up my hope and my situation is improving.

I could not help but notice that the atmosphere in that first renal clinic had become similar to that of a funeral parlor. However, the elderly man from East India was a bright light. He wanted to show us the way he is improving his situation. He wanted to show us Yoga positions which would help.

Everyone has so much to learn in this situation. I refused to let my hope dissipate into depression. I have also started yoga.

Sarah, the social worker, phoned the next day. She was kind and helpful, and I expressed my anger and my thoughts to her. With some indignation I told her I thought it was completely unfair to snuff out hope in favor of medical statements which are based on observations from the outside.

Long ago, in 1956, I received my RN certification. For 35 years I worked as part of the medical profession. Because I had witnessed many miracles which people had made on their own, despite the death pronouncements made by some medical professional, I left the profession and went into recreational therapy, to help people get their minds off their illnesses and focus on something more positive and healing.

I believe that hope, and a positive outlook, as well as prayer and a solid belief system can overrule any human diagnosis. This was definitely stressed by Sarah the social worker at the renal clinic. I believe in preventative medicine, alternative medicine and many other aspects of the healing profession, not just the medical model. I believe one should fight the fear of disease, rather than become the disease. This is easier said than done, because when other infections invade the person, it is difficult to discern whether the secondary infection is just what it is, a secondary infection, or whether it is a new manifestation of the chronic dis-ease. So one must constantly fight the chronic problemfear as well as a new fear brought on by the secondary infection, in order to keep living a healthy, positive life. That is why one's practitioners are an absolute necessity.

What happened to my sister-in-law in the United States, was an example of the "old way" of following the direction of only one healing profession, in her case, the medical tradition.

Henrietta was a sweet and loving person and the world has lost a valiant soul when she died. She and my husband Ray came from Minnesota, and later moved to Arizona.

She had the same afflictions and complaints which apparently I have. She was a very tiny and vibrant little lady and I loved her dearly.

It is said that when she was a tiny baby she was so small they put her into a bureau drawer beside the bed. She stayed there for months so her mother could feed her and keep an eye on her so that she was safe. Henrietta remained small all her life, weighing in adulthood just more than 100 pounds. I knew "Henry" when we were both in our late 60s and she had a wonderful sense of humor. We laughed at the same things and had a good relationship. (Because of her history, I wondered if she had some degree of allergy to wheat all her life.)

Being a good cook, she began working in a high-school cafeteria when her health was good.

She and my husband, Ray, were born on a farm and their mother kept an immense garden which fed the family during the summer and the preserves from the garden lasted through the winter. Their food was mostly preservative free. The tortillas that Henry would make at the high school were made of wheat.

She began having health problems when she was around 70 and, at first, attributed it to getting older. Her complaints were vague - bloating, constipation, pains around her heart and indications of gastric or intestinal ulcer. She was tired all the time. As time went on her complaints grew more frequent, but remained vague.

She was sent to emergency with severe pain around her heart, yet they could not find any cause or heart problem. The doctors were trying everything to help her. She was given medication for this and that ailment.

Initially, she seemed to respond to the treatment, but then would develop something else. This went on for two more years, with several emergency admissions to the hospital for complaints of pains around her heart, abdominal distress, as well as transient ischemic attacks or TIAs, often called mini strokes.

Her system was obviously failing, almost like she was rejecting something. Fortunately for Henrietta, her son, Dennis, came to live with her and took charge of her health and welfare.

He was a saint. He took her back and forth to all her appointments, took her shopping when she had the energy and, after one of her strokes, he protected her from herself, since she had developed such impatience and lack of judgment .

One doctor said he thought she had cancer. They did tests and a tiny lesion of cancer was found in the small intestine. Henrietta was losing weight

Her health insurance company stopped coverage because she was costing them too much money. She went to another health insurance company which meant finding another doctor. She had been ill for two years, without anyone finding the real reason for her problem. As it turned out, the first insurance company's decision to discharge her was a lucky break.

The new doctor diagnosed her with an allergy to wheat (gluten Intolerance) and her health began to improve. With gluten or wheat intolerance, people develop symptoms of heart problems, small intestine problems and live with constant nausea, bloating and either constipation or diarrhea. The hemoglobin becomes low and often the liver function, too. People get very tired and also depressed easily.

Henrietta became very depressed. Her weight fell to 73 pounds. Doctors put her on high-protein milkshakes which she said did not agree with her. The milk shakes made her nauseated. (Often people with gluten intolerance are also intolerant to milk. Therefore it surprised me that the doctors had ordered milk shakes.) Henrietta gradually began to take matters into her own hands. She ate less and less, and eventually stopped eating. When she died, she weighed only 60 pounds.

Doctors of acupuncture and naturopathic healing give time, support and encouragement. They told me that keeping a positive spirit is the most important aspect in healing. The naturopathic doctors know a great deal about the affect of food on the body. They have given me hope. How I wish the medical profession, and the alternate healing professions, could work together to help people. There is so much knowledge to be shared, and no one has all the answers.

When in Wal-Mart getting a prescription filled, the pharmacist asked me about allergies. I mentioned gluten allergy. The lady waiting behind me stopped me a few minutes later and told me she, too, had a gluten allergy. Her name was Lucinda Carver and she had a terrible time with weight.

"I was over 300 pounds, and went into a coma," she told me. "I was close to death when they tried a gluten allergy diagnosis." Lucinda is a fairly tall, good-looking woman who weighs about 150 pounds now. She was an angel in disguise for me and maybe for all the many people in North America who have been diagnosed as obese or morbidly obese. Her story is similar to Henrietta's in that the medical model missed the problem until it was almost too late.

In defense of the medical model, I know the doctors and nurses do their best. Medicine is based on science. I believe there is much more to healing than science, although science is important. However I think science is only part of the equation. The rest of the healing equation has to do with other healing professions as well as the clients own hope and belief system.

I don't know why the fact that my kidneys were failing was missed until it was so late. Perhaps they didn't know about it, since I look so healthy. One reason was that high blood pressure affects the kidneys. My episode with shingles might also have been a contributing factor. High blood pressure was something which both my parents had, and

I also have. The doctors say it can be genetic. There are medicines to combat high blood pressure and I am very grateful for them.

The one thing to keep in mind is to enjoy each day that is given, and to keep positive.

Therefore, just concentrating on the *now* of life and enjoying it is imperative. For an example, my daughter, Laura, took me to a spa and I received a pedicure. That was soooo nice for many reasons. I cannot see well enough to reach my toes properly and the attention given me with the pedicure made me wish to go to sleep; it was so relaxing.

The second renal clinic meeting was much more positive. They still were pointing us all in the direction of dialysis, but made the prospect more acceptable by showing us dialysis machines we could use in our homes.

Friends of ours have a son-in-law who had been given a transplant. His name is Michael Williams and he is so supportive and encouraging to me and I still lean on him heavily.

For example, I was told at the clinic that transplant cutoff is 60 and I'm going on 75. He suggested I ask about "extended criteria donors," where acceptable organs for older donors are given to recipients of a similar age.

There remains one niggling question in my mind, which I asked Dr. Hargrave at my last visit: "If I was to receive a kidney from a person who was a "wheat eater" would I reject the kidney, or would it kill me?" Dr. Hargrave was very honest and replied: "It's a good question and I don't know the answer."

In the meantime, I attended the Back to Back Clinic and saw Drs. Rabnett and Morrison every other week.

Dr. Rabnett offered a "reconnection" treatment which I accepted. Reconnection Healing links us to the energies of the Universe and it was then I began to become aware of a healing energy which I call the "Ancients."

How can I explain this phenomenon? There are many of them. They are shapeless in form. Their shapes and color change, like their shapes fluctuate in and out or back and forth. They are grey, sometimes black and sometimes almost transparent. I wonder if the change in color is because they are absorbing some of the toxins built up in my system. All I do know is that they are pure healing energy. They do not socialize, they heal. That's their job.

Many skeptical readers will say I am crazy. I am not. I simply was able to communicate with them. When I took the treatment I didn't know what to expect. Dr. Eric Pearl said it all in his book, The Reconnection," and I quote:

"If you're lucky, your healing will come in the form you anticipate. If you're really lucky, your healing will come in a form you've not even dreamed of—one the Universe specifically has in mind for you."

I looked "reconnective healing" up in the Internet and it said the following:

"Reconnective healing links us to the energies of the Universe, as it joins us to the awareness of our beings. It utilizes new frequencies that help to bring a shift to all levels of the body, mind and spirit. Reconnective Healing is healing by reconnecting the grid system of light/energy of the body and the DNA."

There seems to be a very quiet shift going on in this old world, away from old beliefs and traditions. The shift involves an awareness of the many energies unseen but definitely felt, which can only be described as the winds of change.

My healing is remarkable and continual. People who had known me before the illness have all remarked on how I was returning to the person I used to be. This kept on until about four months later, when I was in church, and something odd happened. I started to wobble and had difficulty lighting a candle and later singing from the hymn book. It seemed so heavy my arms couldn't hold it. I whispered to Ray that something was wrong and we left the church.

He took me to the emergency department at the Victoria General Hospital. My limbs continued to move involuntarily and in a more severe manner. My speech was slow and slurred and I felt like I was on a "high," like a happy drunk. I saw several nurses, one of whom started me on an intravenous of fluid with sodium. The blood tests showed my sodium and potassium were too low. That didn't surprise me since I had been stringent with both by omitting foods high in them from my diet.

My outer body became very cold. I lay very still in order to quiet my limbs, which were moving uncontrollably. It was then that I became aware that I was rising above my body. I also became aware that I had no specific shape. I was shapeless energy like the Ancients. Then I became aware of their presence working on my body below. Someone came into the cubicle and also began working on my feet. It was a woman, and I thought to myself: "This hospital is really advanced when they send in human healers to help the patients."

I asked aloud: "Are you a healer?" She answered: "Yes, I am a healer." Those hands moved up my body and reached my head; then long hair fell over my face and a warm cheek rested on mine while the "healer" whispered and sobbed: "I am Laura!" We both wept. Laura is my daughter.

She told me she was going to bring me back into my body. I told her it was really strange to be in two places at once.

A neurological doctor by the name of John came and gave me several tests. Dr. John is tall, lanky, good looking with blue eyes that sparkle and an expression which said, "Trust me. I know what I'm doing."He was from the military, on loan to the hospital. He was also one of the warmest most personable doctors I have ever met.

They sent me for a CT scan. I could hardly get from the stretcher onto the table, my limbs were so uncooperative, but I finally managed to roll over onto that table. Upon my return they continued to give me the intravenous fluid and evaluate me again.

My speech was beginning to clarify and I was more aware of my surroundings again. However, I was still on that "high" and loved the whole world.

Later, Dr. John and Dr. Sun, the head of the emergency unit, came and talked to me. Dr. Sun reminded me of the harpist I met in Peru. He is very solid in build, with dark eyes and a nice big smile.

He is careful in speech and very thorough. He perseveres until he has all the information he needs. They thought I had experienced a TIA. They made an appointment for me to have an ultrasound and to see a neurologist. They tested me to see if I could walk, and I could, with some help, although only a few baby steps.

My co-ordination, however, was returning and I was feeling stronger. They discharged me.

When home, I received a call from Dr. Sun asking a bit about what I was eating and drinking and I told him about adding no salt, eating foods containing as little sodium and potassium as possible because of my kidneys and a gluten-free diet because of the wheat allergy. He said to drink more juices and have a soda once or twice a week to bring the electrolytes back up. He called on a Sunday afternoon. Now that is an example of a concerned doctor.

The next morning a little after 9 a.m., I received another call, this one from the ultrasound department. They asked that I come for an appointment. Then another agency called. It was the stroke-assessment office to tell me they wished to see me after I had the ultrasound. I would be seeing the neurologist at that time.

Time seemed to be a foreign dimension. My memory for short-term events seemed completely gone. I wrote everything down, made lists and put the appointments on the calendar before I forgot them.

My friend, Sharon, took me around to the appointments. I don't remember much about the ultrasound, but I do remember the appointment with the neurologist, Dr. Kristen Attwell-Pope. She told me she had read the ultrasound and CT scans and that I had experienced a stroke. She also said it probably wasn't the first one.

I remembered that about three years earlier – when I was so sick with shingles – my limbs became completely uncoordinated and after that I went to "la- la land," where I met my mom, dad, sister and brother who had all passed through the veil of life and death, and they told me: "Go Back! Your work is not completed!"

Awhile after the stroke, I started to bleed, I guess from the kidney, and passed a small stone. That was another real experience in pain.

As I write this, I have learned that I have the right to question, suggest and choose what is right for me. I believe I'm going to improve my health and I've already done so. I have made myself the head of a very knowledgeable and positive team that is assembled to help me.

I take a very active part in accepting what I think is good for me, questioning and discarding that which doesn't work. I've become very verbal with all my practitioners. After all, I live in this body.

There is another gift I am receiving from all this. I am learning to count my blessings and grow upwards. Here's an example: I'm learning more patience with myself and with others. I'm learning to see the funny side to everything. Laughter in itself is healing.

With the help of our Canadian British Columbia health insurance, Dr. Gaylene Hargrave, my nephrologist, Dr. Kristen Attwell-Pope, my neurologist, Dr. Jim Saffrey, my GP in Victoria, B.C., Dr. Gregory Porter, my internal specialist in Tucson, Drs. Stefan Rabnett and Kyle Morrison, my alternative healing doctors, Dr. Sun and staff of the Victoria general emergency staff, along with all the medications and gluten free diet, I am healing.

An interesting postscript to all of this is that my daughter, Laura, took me to a psychic interpreter, a lady by the name of Kitty Lloyd in Nanaimo, B.C., north of Victoria. She had never seen me before. Among many other things, she told me I will live until I'm 98 and my third book will be published when I'm 92. (Kitty Lloyd has since retired.)

I am maintaining that positive attitude and have now almost completed this, my first book. The Spirit of Dis--ease is teaching me to believe in myself, to use all of the powers in our Universe to help me on my journey. Each day is more valuable than the last and brings more gifts of great value. I am also immensely grateful to my own personal Spirits, who represent our Universal God and who praise the name of our God in every act of goodness. I have also learned to take better care of this beautiful temple called the body, and to slow down and balance my mind, body and spirit. I have learned very clearly that the physical body is just as important as the intellect, and spirit, and is not to be taken for granted.

Spirit runs through all our lives and helps us to live our most honorable selves. Our Spirit connects us to the great Universe and joins us to our Maker. I pray that you will enjoy your Sacred Spirit as much as I am enjoying mine, and that each day will bring you treasures from the Universe to help you make a difference in your worlds. All you have to do is ask.

CHAPTER 22

The Spirit of Reiki, a Healing Energy

Your health is a unique point of balance between your mind, your body and your soul – We all have within us healing Spiritual energy.- DorisMae Honer

The medical model of healing rests on science. This has always interested me, and healing has been something I am drawn to like a magnet. The fact that there are many other healing modalities is something else which is fascinating. This is why I became drawn to the healing energy of the Reiki practice.

When Jesus healed the sick, the lame, the deaf and the blind, he didn't give them pills. He used his own holy energy from God. Where did he learn all this? I believe he and his family fled to India when they were being persecuted. Did he learn the many healing modalities there? Or did he always have them since he was the Son of God?

We are told we are made in the image of God, that we are all children of God. If this is true, and I believe it to be, then we have within us a healing energy if we wish to use it. Therefore, I began my quest to find the healing energy which I could use to help people heal. When my late husband Bryan and I arrived in Tucson, in 1996, I asked my friend Billie Baty to teach me the three ascending levels of Reiki, and with much study and practice, I became a Reiki master.

How does one explain Reiki? It is the laying on of hands, like

Jesus did when he was on earth. My Reiki instructor told me that even if my client came and did not feel or believe that healing was taking place, it still would take place. The healing is an energy which comes through the healer to the client. The healing comes from the Universe and the person with healing hands is merely a conduit.

Many people came to me with physical problems and I did what I could using the methodology as I had learned in my classes. Sometimes my clients went to sleep and had dreams or visions. Some shared them with me. They saw colors and places almost forgotten from their youth. Sometimes I had visions relating to the client's lives during the sessions.

Most of my clients went on "journeys" and came back to earth when the healing session was over. I recorded my findings from my own visions, as well as the clients' experiences in a journal. I remember several clients to this day without having to check my journal. These episodes were truly gifts from God, giving me a glimpse into eternity. Two of the names of my clients have been changed to protect their confidentiality.

Sara:

Sara called me after hearing about me through a friend. She had a physical complaint which was vague, something she could not understand. I knew nothing of Sara's past life, only that she wanted to rid herself of the vague but perpetual pain for which doctors had never found a cause.

As I worked on Sara's body, all seemed well until I put my hands on part of her side. I was given a vision of old, grey dried up tissue. I also heard a faint baby's cry. I continued on and all seemed well in all other parts of Sara, with the exception of this one part. I heard the baby cry again.

"Sara," I said. "There is a baby spirit around you. The baby wishes to be recognized. Will you reach out in your mind and hold the baby, and tell the baby he is loved?"

I continued to put my Reiki hands on that part of Sara's side.

Sara began to weep. I could feel the energy flowing through my hands. It made my hands hot, almost like fire.

Sara lay very still and I told her that the baby had stopped crying. The dead grey tissue in my vision had turned to the most beautiful soft yellow brightness and I knew Sara had healed.

When the healing session finished, Sara told me she had lost a baby through a miscarriage a long time ago. She told me that in her mind she had reached out and held her baby and it made her feel so much better to know he was safe. She told her baby that she loved him. When she left, she appeared relaxed and happy. I never heard from her again. I know she was healed and so too was that lonely little baby boy spirit.

Ralph: ━━━━━━━━━━━━━━━━━━━━━━━━━

Ralph was a neighbor who was having trouble relaxing because of many worries. Ralph is his real name. As I worked on him, Ralph was able to see different energies in color. First he saw very dark colors of blacks, browns, swirling and turning grey, then purple growing lighter like a band from the rainbow, joined by more beautiful greens blues and finally the soft bright yellows. I have wondered if the colors represented different stresses he was carrying inside and that as he healed, the changing colors marked changing energies.

He left the session feeling much more relaxed. I went away for quite awhile, but saw Ralph again a few years later. He now has his own business. He has joined a community of very loving people and is well accepted by all in his world. Ralph still mentions his Reiki session and is appreciative of God's energies.

Eva: ━━━━━━━━━━━━━━━━━━━━━━━━━━

Eva was referred to me by her doctor. She was terminally ill with cancer and he said he could not increase her pain medicine since she was at the limit of what he could prescribe. Eva came to me in a wheel chair, pushed by her nurse.

We both helped Eva up onto the table, and I explained to her about Reiki. The nurse waited for her in the waiting room. As I worked on Eva's body, I felt her begin to relax. By the end of the session she had relaxed so much she said the pain was much less than it had been.

She asked if she could come back and we made another appointment for the following week.

The next week she came walking into the Reiki room. Her nurse was still with her and waited in the waiting room. The Reiki session was uneventful, I simply did what I was supposed to do and saw Eva relaxing as she had in the first session. Then she fell asleep, before I had finished. This made me smile, in wonder and appreciation at God's healing energy.

She continued to visit once a week, and each time she came I could feel her energy increasing. She mentioned that she wanted to go and visit her brother in a different state and hoped she would regain enough energy to take the plane. She also mentioned that she had cut down on her pain medication considerably. The last session we had together was amazing. Eva went to sleep as usual.

As I worked healing Reiki hands over her body I had a vision. Eva was sitting under a huge tree at the edge of a field, and there was a German shepherd dog beside her with his head in her lap as she petted him. They both looked content as they sat there under the shade of the big tree. When Eva awakened at the end of the treatment, I told her of my vision. She said, "That was my dog when I was little. I loved him so much, and he loved me back the same way. A neighbor shot him. I've never gotten over it."

I asked Eva if she believed in the Spirit world. She said she did. I asked her if by any chance her dog's spirit had come to tell her he was OK and that he loved her. Eva didn't say much but she smiled. Her next appointment was cancelled because she had taken a plane to see her brother.

Bryan:

Bryan was my late husband. He was an intelligent and sensitive man. I loved him very much. While he was alive, but failing, from many chronic Illnesses, we both knew that each day we had together was a real blessing. Four years ago he had been told he had six weeks to six months to live. We had moved to the sunny south where he regained much of his energy, and with the help of Dr. Porter, and the dry Arizona weather, his life changed and he even started a business there. However, four years passed and the illnesses were ravaging his body and he was failing physically. He asked me to give him Reiki.

Initially Reiki helped Bryan relax, and he was able to sleep and be more comfortable. Bryan told me he knew he wasn't going to be around much longer. Apparently he was worried about several parts of his life in which he had not evoked closure. The three last Reiki sessions are memorable, and to me are messages from beyond the veil. The first of the three last sessions were described by Bryan clearly. "I was walking through a beautiful tunnel. The walls were made of red velvet, and at the end of the tunnel were beautiful oak doors. They had panes of glass in them and when I got to the doors, I looked through the windows but I couldn't see anything. I tried to open the doors but they were locked. So I came back." I asked him what he thought this meant and he responded, "I have to finish some things I've left undone." I asked him how he was going to do this and he responded that he didn't know how.

The second of the three sessions was similar, as far as I was concerned; I had no visions nor saw any colors. I just did my Reiki job as I had been taught. However, when Bryan described his experience I was amazed.

He recounted: "I went back into the tunnel, but this time it was filled with smoke. I could see the doors were still locked, and I came back." Again I asked if he knew what the smoke meant, and he answered that he had not attended to closure of something in his past. "I don't know how to do it. I know what I want to say, but I feel so helpless and don't know what to do."

We decided that he would dictate what he wanted to say and I would write it down for him. After this was done, we crumpled the letter up, put it into a large shallow clay dish, and lit it on fire as we said a prayer, that the spirit of the letter would be heard by its intended.

The next Reiki session was as usual for me, and when it ended Bryan said that he had gone through the tunnel, which was filled with light. At the end of the tunnel the doors were open, and covered by a beautiful soft yellow sheer curtain. He could see through the curtain and said, "There were so many people there all waving and happy." Bryan went to sleep that night, and I was awakened during the night to see a very bright radiant figure about 4foot seven or eight walking noiselessly around the room. She approached the sleeping Bryan, and then disappeared. Three days later Bryan graduated to the next kingdom. Although he has gone from earth, I know he is busy helping our Father in heaven with the environment of earth, which was his greatest love. Love never dies. It just gets transferred from one person or one place to the next kingdom.

CHAPTER 23

The Different Faces of Love

Your daily life is your temple and your religion. Whenever you enter in to it take with you your all - The Prophet Khahil Gibran on religion

I call this episode channeling a conversation between my Higher Spirit and me.

This is taken from one of my journals, where I write to my guides, to God and to my own indwelling Spirit, when I am puzzled about something and seek an answer. Many people do the same thing, and I'm delighted to read that more and more people are connecting with their Spirits by writing to them.

I wrote the following to Spirit:

What does love mean to you?

Is love what you hear sung about in ballads from the time you were able to understand words? Is love just a feeling?

Spirit: *I think that love is a totally encompassing feeling.*

Me: All right, a "feeling." That's a good starting point. Then does love come from without or within? You say both? Can you please enlarge that for me?

Spirit: *I think a feeling of love starts with warmth, nurturing and well being. You experienced this first when you were the infant floating in your Mother's womb. You experienced the warmth then, from another, and it began with and from your Mother who held you within herself. Interesting, she was experiencing "Within" while you were experiencing "Without". Therefore you and Mother were "at one" with yourselves, both "within" and "without."*

Me: That sounds a little confusing but I understand and agree. I'd like to look closer at the "at-one" concept, as in the mother experiencing within and child without.

Spirit: *This is one of nature's miracles, and holds many small miracles within the evolution of one life into two. Generally speaking love is one of the most important feelings which come from the start of this Nature's miracle. A man and a woman combine to make a new life. Although most of the time this is done in a loving way, there are also times when an intrusive and less than honorable action, like rape, produces the new life. This should not impact the new life, although many times the new life is terminated because of this action.*

Me: I'm not sure what you mean by "not impacting the new life." For myself, if I had to face the prospect of rape and then realize I had become pregnant, I would probably be inclined to wish the growing life away, because it had started without my consent.

Spirit: *I hear your concern. However, let me remind you about Martha, a lady we both know and love. What happened to Martha, and how she lived is legend in the Spirit world. Her story is a pure and true one, and although the details may inflame some people, nevertheless, let's examine her life.*

MARTHA: A NOBLE SPIRIT.

Martha had been walking home from school. It was late and she was hurrying. She was a very pretty young woman of 16 and the time was nearing the end of the Second World War. Her country had been invaded by the German army, but the Americans had come to liberate the people in her village.

Martha was stopped by two American soldiers who were driving an army truck. They asked directions and Martha hopped into the truck to help them, since her English was quite good. She had studied English in school and hoped to become a teacher. Unfortunately, Martha became the victim of rape, before she was dropped off, tearful and completely broken, on her mother's doorstep.

As time went on Martha's body healed from the experience, but both she and her Mother began to realize that she had been impregnated.

When Martha was 17, she delivered a beautiful dark-skinned baby girl.

Martha completed her education and taught in a local elementary school for many years, while living with her parents and her baby girl.

To keep anonymity, let's call the baby Rose.

Rose was an adorable and loving, gentle little girl who had dark skin and African American features. She loved to play with her little homemade dolls, and was also loving and gentle with the family pets. She grew up and went into Nurse's Training, because she wanted to help people, and especially to help heal the sick and injured. She graduated and moved to the United States to study further, and while there met and married a young man in the military. They had several children.

Martha met and married a Finish-Canadian man she had met when he was on vacation, and later she moved to Canada, to start a new life in the province of Ontario, with her mining man.

Each year on Martha's birthday, Rose, her husband and their children came to visit with Martha in Northern Ontario, Canada. They respected and loved Martha with a love which can only be described as sacred.

They all knew so deeply in their souls, that without Martha's bravery in the face of great adversity, they would not have been granted Life.

Martha is an example of the large picture or dimension of life. She lived beyond the small circle of her own wishes. She took the little life within her, loved that life into reality, and was blessed many *fold by her actions. Martha was loved by many during her stay on earth, and is well loved by all in the Spirit World.*

Me: I remember Martha. I got to know her well, and helped to take care of her during her final years. I also met her American family. I have always remembered her, loved her and respected her bravery, and the love of the people who visited her yearly.

Spirit: *Let's count up the words which describe Martha. Warmth, gentleness, love, respect, caring, positive action when faced with adversity, bravery and courage, believing in the greater good for all concerned. Would you say these words also describe love? Do you know of any other great people who have lived on this planet who could be described in the same way?*

Me: Yes. Jesus Christ, Mohammed, the Dalai Lama, Mother Theresa, Gandhi, Nelson Mandela, and many simply beautiful people I have met who are giving of themselves and are honorable.

Thank you Spirit for your wisdom and insight and allowing me to see the bigger pictures in life.

CHAPTER **24**

The Magic of Spirit

Life has taught us that love does not consist in gazing at each other, but in looking outward together in the same direction - Antoine de Saint- Exupery, French writer and aviator.

Alan A. Cohen wrote a book titled Handle with Prayer: Harnessing the Power to Make Your Dreams Through. In the book, he advised: "Quit trying to run the show. Let your Spirit help you."

Later he says: "We think in Spirit and it comes to pass. Environment is our mirror."

A long time ago a doctor told me: "You attract what you need." I didn't believe him at that time, but I sure do now.

I think being thankful and saying so out loud is important. It's important to you, to the person who has given something to you and it's important to God and the Universe. Many poets and authors say that's so because we are all so interconnected.

Respect is also important to Spirit. By respect, I mean respecting you and your own power; respecting and following through on your responsibilities, respecting Spirit, as well as everyone else's individuality and power. Respect is shown in the voice, in the tone of love, facial expression and body language. As a matter of fact, disrespect shows up the same way.

No one can get away with anything but truth. If our words belie our intention, that voice of ours will give us away every time.

Magic shows up in all sorts of mediums. Music, according to Michael Newton, is the language of the Gods (Destiny of Souls: New Case Studies In Life Between Lives, pg. 304-305; California Press, California).

The magic in music can soothe the soul. Depending on the type of music heard, it can also send the Spirit spinning to get away.

We find the Magic of Spirit in the most unusual places, like, for instance, in an argument. When we are confronted, instead of being defensive, the honest admission of thoughts and feelings defuses the argument immediately. In other words, the best defense is no defense. Here's an example:

A well-loved person by the name of Ken was confronted by his enraged friend, Paul, who couldn't understand why, in his words; Ken had made such a "gross" mistake. Ken understood the world of Spirit, but he knew his friend Paul was still closed. Therefore Ken used the term "gut" in his explanation, rather than Spirit, so that Paul could understand and accept his explanation.

Ken's reply was this: "This is the way it was with me. I was feeling uncertain and there wasn't anyone around to advise me. So I bumbled along and did what my gut (Spirit) told me to do and trusted that everything would turn out all right."

As it turned out, when the final assessment was completed, Ken had made the right decisions. He had also disarmed the confronting Paul, without malice.

The Magic of Spirit lies in many places. Firstly, we are told that the past must be let go. Khahil Gibran writes in his book, The Prophet: "The moving finger writes, and having writ moves on and all your tears and all your fears will not change a word of it."

My mom used to say: "If you make a mistake, don't fret. You'll get another chance to rectify it, because life always gives you the same situation dressed up in a different dress, until you finally learn the lesson." She also cautioned me that critics were "angels in disguise."

Abraham Lincoln always valued his critics and listened intently to what was said, and benefited from the truth that was in the criticism.

That boils down to the bottom line, which is truth.

Ken spoke his own truth, followed the directions of his Spirit, and the result was positive.

It seems like the Spirit demands truth and evokes its magic when we live our lives being positive in attitude, having faith, hope, trust and respect for self and all others and treating our world with openness and with love in our hearts.

Learning to speak one's truth should be as simple as it sounds. But is it?

Have any of us been taught that we should withhold our own thoughts and be polite? Children often speak their truth, and a shocked parent hushes them up. Has that ever happened to you?

My mother was entertaining her friends in our living room one afternoon. They had come for tea. I remember she brought me in to meet the ladies. I was just a toddler at the time and was absolutely awed by the face of one particular woman. She was smiling in a friendly way but I kept staring at her in absolute wonder. My mom asked me what I was thinking. Pointing at her friend, I told her the lady had a face like a small monkey. Mom rushed me out of the room and told me I was very impolite. All I knew was that she did look like a monkey to me. I had learned about the monkeys from pictures my sister Margaret showed me. That was my truth at the time. As I grew I learned to pick and choose what to say that was polite and to keep some of my truths to myself. Learning to speak one's truth probably takes time and a good connection with one's inner Spirit, the real person we are under all the layers of learned diversion to the real truth.

As an adult, I've found that working to find oneself in all those layers we have learned from various authority figures takes time. It took time to develop those layers; it will take time to peel them away. One must develop new perspectives and expend much thought and effort in the process. One must learn to replace the ego with humility, a large dose of humility. I think that is what Jesus meant when he said that we entered the kingdom of heaven as children. I think he meant that we had to outgrow egotism, deceit, false beliefs in power, and we had to replace all that with honesty and truth.

The leaders of our countries are supposed to lead with honor. But do they? A war was waged with Iraq over "weapons of mass destruction" only to find there were none. It seems like the news media is often guilty of leading the masses with fear and sensationalism.

How different and ugly is the world as described by the media, when it focuses mostly on the negative. A sage once told me that whatever we focus on gets bigger, and whatever we ignore gets smaller.

The world we make for ourselves is so different from the world as described on the TV news, and in the newspapers. If we focus on the Spiritual, it gets bigger, and the negative worldly events diminish in their value in our minds. Although the shift which is occurring in people's minds hasn't hit any headlines, people are definitely changing from followers to independent thinkers.

Mike Dooley, in his book Infinite Possibilities: The Art of Living Your Dreams, writes: "Anything which affects our thinking affects our lives. And nothing else affects our thinking more than our beliefs. Our beliefs shape our thoughts and our world."

By letting our Spirit help us, as Alan Cohen suggests, we will touch upon real truth, we will ascend to higher levels of thought and deed. We will grow upwards then with our Spirit, like a spiral, going round and round, forever climbing, until we reach the very face of God.

CHAPTER **25**

A Spirit Closes the Circle of Love

Louise Barry Rose is a wonderful, sensitive, open hearted and intelligent woman with deep understanding of people, nature and the world. She is also a very creative lady who plays the piano and organ and decorates her church in a very artistic, pleasing way. She has been an editor for a small newspaper and writes beautifully.

Her husband, Frank, is a retired minister, an artist and a man whose empathy towards people helps them to heal. He is also a deep thinker. I have admired both Louise and Frank for many years and count them as my friends.

Louise has written an extensive history about baby Charles for her family and shared it with me. As I read it I was deeply moved. With Louise's permission, I have taken parts of the story to include in this book so my readers may know both Louise and Charles and share in the miracle given to Louise.

Baby Charles

Where there is great love, there are always miracles - Willa Cather, author, Pulitzer Prize winner 1922

The family was living in Colchester, England, at the time and had been there for several years. Their five children were all under the age of eight. Louise admits she was a little "grumpy" on Christmas

Day when she learned that she was expecting another baby. Her pregnancy left her tired and she admits that when the pregnancy became a certainty, she found it difficult to remain pleasant and calm all the time.

Frank was a busy minister and on August 6, 1964, he and his brother, Don, were away from their home running the British Academy Summer School. This was a highly successful summer school for church students who came from the US, South Africa, England, Scotland, Sweden, Denmark, France and other parts of Europe. Each year, the pastors in England would find a boarding school to rent for two weeks during the summer. This year the school had been located in Watford, about two hours away from Colchester.

When Louise went for her routine visit to her obstetrician, she was feeling a little apprehensive since her regular doctor - who Louise described as a caring man with all his patients - was on vacation. The doctor filling in was described by Louise as a "cold fish doctor who was very smart, but with no charisma at all."

Because of her unusual abdominal distension, he took X-rays, but could not define the size of the baby because of the abnormal amount of fluid. He decided Louise was to be admitted to the Colchester Maternity Hospital.

This came as a shock to Louise, but she was allowed to return to her home and make preparations for the admission. Frank's mother, affectionately called Ma, was visiting their home and helping with the children while Frank and Don were in summer school.

Don's wife, Noelene, and her two children were also visiting the Rose family and helping with the children.

Louise is a very observant lady and an excellent writer. Her observations and descriptions of the hospital, staff, and happenings were as follows:

"The head nurse in the maternity hospital was a large, discontented-looking woman. She was the boss and therefore it might be appropriate for her to be bossy, but I noticed that she was rubbing everyone the wrong way. The nurses who were the targets of her constant commands spoke as little as possible to her and rolled their eyes at each other when she wasn't looking. I called that head nurse "Big Nurse" inside my head."

Louise's story continues: "I had been in the ward for several hours and I guess Big Nurse wanted some action. The nurses helped me into a hospital gown and asked me to lie down on the delivery table.

"It's time to break her waters," barked Big Nurse. This was done by one of the nurses, and Louise was drenched.

"Now I want you to stand up and walk to the bathroom," Big Nurse ordered Louise sternly. The bathroom was about 20 yards down the hall and Louise steadied herself against the wall as she made her barefoot way toward that cold little cubicle. She was shivering when she felt the first mild contraction come on.

On returning, using the corridor wall for balance, the hospital staff had a dry gown and a bed with wheels waiting for her. The delivery room was cavernous, all white, with her bed in the center. She felt exposed and unprotected. She glanced at the clock. Nightfall was close at hand.

The ceiling rose in slanting lines to a skylight high above. She had lain there for several hours with the contractions coming closer and closer. Louise had requested that the staff refrain from giving her anesthetic. The first four Rose babies had been born at home with no anesthetic at all.

A nurse came in from time to time to check on her progress. For Louise, that night was long, dark, painful and lonely. As time went on she could see through the skylight that the darkness was beginning to be tinged with the gentle colors of dawn; soft shades of pink, yellow and blue which helped to soothe her. As the contractions continued, she said that the dawning day seemed to be sending her a silent blessing, a reassuring message of comfort and hope.

She began to pray: "Our Father who art in heaven . . . ." She pictured Frank and her beautiful children and realized once again how much each beautiful face meant to her.

Suddenly, the morning nurses burst into the room, noisy, joking with each other, poking her with cold fingers and exclaiming at her progress. Big Nurse appeared, snapping orders and taking control. Above Louise, the sky was now pure blue. The day had come.

Louise delivered the baby that morning.

She writes: "Of the six times I've given birth, this was the easiest. I kept waiting for the grueling part of the delivery, the part that made women call it labor, but it never came. I heard a gasp from the nurses and a soft pitiful cry from the baby. Someone said, 'It's a boy.' My fifth boy, I thought to myself.

"This baby looks premature," cried Big Nurse with a panicky edge to her voice. "Mrs. Rose, when did you conceive?

"How on earth could I remember a thing like that at a moment like this? Under her breath, Big Nurse said, 'Give her a shot.'

"They stuck a needle in my leg just as I turned to see my son. The moment I saw him I fell in love with him. He was adorable. His little eyes were blinking, his dark hair matted on his head. He was rather blue and making low grunting sounds. The nurses were holding him up for me to see and it was then I began to notice what the certificate later referred to as 'multiple congenital deformities.' I saw that his arms stopped just below the elbow and there became little boneless, malformed hands. I saw that his legs below the knees seemed to bend in ways that were not possible.

"Whatever they gave me in that shot began to take effect. My head was full of fog and dizziness swirling around inside."

Louise continues: "there seemed to be a lot of hurrying and urgent voices. I struggled to get my brain clear enough to think. I did not know then that I would never see my baby again. In the absence of thought, all I could do was feel. A wave of feeling would wash over me knocking me off balance like an undertow that was going to drown me. Then all would gradually wash away leaving only peace and trust. The panic would build up again quickly and would break over me like a bucket of water thrown in my face. If only my mind would clear!"

As time went on, Louise asked the nurses to call her home and let her mother-in-law know what was happening. "I'm sorry we can't do that," was their answer. "The maternity hospital has a strict policy that we only speak to the father of the baby with details about his birth." Louise could not get in touch with Frank because the phone number was at home in Colchester. She asked them to phone her home and get the number, and received the answer: "Don't worry dear we'll take care of it."

Big Nurse came in with an urgent request for Louise to name the child so he could be baptized by a Church of England clergyman they had on staff. "He may not live," she said intently. "So you must have him baptized. What name do you have for him?" Frank and Louise had not even discussed names this time. Louise's head was so groggy. However, she said the name Charles floated into her head and that was the name she chose. Big Nurse hurried out to have it taken care of.

Louise continued: "Suddenly, three doctors appeared at the foot of the bed and began asking question after question." Louise said she felt like she was being drilled.

They asked when she had conceived Charles, the ages of her other children and what medications she was taking.

Louise says her mind was still sluggish. As the questioning continued, a nurse came into the room and spoke softly into Louise's ear. "By the way, Mrs. Rose, the baby is gone."

Louise turned her face to the wall and would not answer any more questions. Tears streamed down her face. She wrote later: "I had so little awareness of what I needed that I did not ask for anything. I did not know that I needed to touch Charles, to hold him and say goodbye." Louise was in a deep state of shock.

Apparently no one suggested that she do this as a final goodbye which would have provided Louise with some comfort and some degree of closure. They moved her into a private room.

Charles had been born at dawn. Eventually the hospital reached Frank and it was late afternoon when Frank arrived to see Louise. Frank comforted Louise and gave her strength after the terrible ordeal. He had to leave again after a short conversation as the hospital had strict rules about visiting. And only fathers were allowed to visit.

Frank was, and still is, a very resourceful man. Before he left Colchester he did something special that made Louise smile and think to herself: "What a man! I am so blest!" Frank had explored around the hospital and figured out how a person could get to Louise's room without going past the nurses' station. Then he drew a little map.

After supper a familiar smiling face appeared in the doorway of her room. Soon Louise was hugging Ma. With great feeling Ma said: "Now you are the mother of an angel!" She had come sneaking into the hospital using Frank's map. Louise was overjoyed to see her. They cried together.

After Louise had been moved into a room by herself following the birth, Big Nurse came in and found her crying. She looked at the photograph on the tray table.

"Who's that?" she asked.

"My little son, Owen," Louise replied, "he's 16 months old."

Big Nurse spoke sternly. "Mrs. Rose, you must not be greedy. You have five other children to take care of. Be content with that."

Louise wondered: "Did she expect me to lose a child and not grieve?"

However, as time went on Louise began to see the truth in what Big Nurse had said. She writes: "I saw that I had five beautiful children to take care of. I did not need to feel deprived for the lack of another. The Lord has blessed me greatly and my cup was running over. "

Baby Charles was buried in the cemetery nearby; on a lovely sunny spot, as Frank described it. The family was able to put a headstone on the spot much later when the demands of their family afforded some money for little Charles.

Time went on and the Rose family seemed to recover from the loss of Charles. In retrospect, Louise said she had simply not known how she was going to cope with a new baby and the demands of her active five children. Although life with the busy family unfolded quickly from day to day, Louise had no time to mourn completely the death of Charles.

Mourning includes the process of dealing with remorse. Louise seemed to be torn between wanting little Charles, with his dark hair and blinking eyes, and being relieved that with all his many deformities, he had been taken from her.

In the mid-1980s Frank and Louise were running a life enrichment group which met in their home. There were about 12 of them sitting in their customary circle, with Frank leading the group in meditation.

Louise writes: "Frank instructed us to close our eyes, breathe deeply, relax completely and clear our minds of all distracting thoughts. I felt myself sink into a serene state where all seemed well and the Lord was near. Frank's voice told us to invite a loved one into that space with us, someone in the past who had been precious to us.

"Before I had time to think about who to invite, Charles appeared before me. He was a tall beautiful young man with glowing soft eyes. I knew at once that it was him and I blurted out, 'Hello Charles, I'm your mother.' He smiled warmly and responded, 'I know that!' as he looked at me with such love in his eyes and in the expression of his face. For a few moments we gazed at each other with adoration, and without words. I felt deeply happy. Then I said, 'I'm sorry I never kissed you to show you I loved you.' He replied, 'I could feel your love around me, even without a kiss.'

"In the presence of this radiant angel, unspoken things were communicated to me; that he knows all our family, he rejoices and grieves with us as we grow through life, and he looks after us tenderly.

"As Charles slowly faded away, and Frank's voice called us back into the room, my heart was full of love and gratitude. I felt weak and glad to be sitting down. I was also tearful, as I usually am when it comes to my son Charles."

In July, 2007, Louise wrote a long, beautiful poem describing her feelings from the time she knew she was pregnant, until she lost her little baby. I want to share with you a verse which especially describes her feelings. This is a small part of that poem as she strives to reach her little baby.

> How could I forget?
> How can I even ask the question?'
> And yet when the tears come
> what I always ask is this:
> Charles my son, do you know how much I love you?

In 2008, after that beautiful vision, Louise Rose said: "it was Charles's smiling reply – 'I know that.' He knows me! He knows I am his mother! And he knows how much I love him!"

In the book, "Soul Light," written by Janna Excel, her guiding Spirit Anna states that some Spirits need only to obtain a body before returning to "home" where God lives. I wonder if Charles was one of those very special Spirits, filled with love, and creating a miracle, by coming back to reassure his mother.

CHAPTER 26

Slow Motion Horror and God Answers Prayers

And if this day is not a fulfillment of your needs and my love, then let it be a promise till another day – The Prophet Khahil Gibran

It was really cold that February day in Montreal. The year was 1958 and I had just found out that I was pregnant. I was working for the Victorian Order of Nurses, and my supervisor, Miss Brandt, handed me a note with the address of a man I was to go and visit. His son had phoned and said there was something wrong with his father and that he had become very ill. The Victorian Order of Nurses is a visiting nurse service which could be accessed at that time by family, relatives and clients themselves as well as the medical profession.

"Stop by on your last call and assess him," she advised me. "Call our doctor and send him to emergency if you think it necessary."

The address wasn't too far from where I lived. It would be a relief to finish the day. I was tired all the time because of the new life within me and more than a little emotional, as well as being somewhat nauseated.

My afternoon clients were all getting along well and I knocked on the new client's door about three in the afternoon. A young man opened it and beckoned me inside.

An older man was sitting in an easy chair and had just put out a cigarette. As I approached him, chatting all the while, I evaluated him briefly. To myself I said: "His color looks good. He's been smoking, he's overweight, but there's no edema in his ankles. His bare feet aren't swollen, he's breathing clearly and without effort, and he seems relaxed."

Taking my coat off, I placed it carefully over a kitchen chair, and placed my bag on the chair's seat. I unzipped the bag, took out my stethoscope and blood pressure cuff before zipping the bag up again. All the while I was chatting about the weather to both men as I approached the older man again. The younger man seemed to be hovering back of me and when I glanced back he was looking intently at my zipped bag.

I stooped down beside the older man and adjusted the blood pressure cuff to his arm, while glancing at his fingernails. They were almost as pink as mine except for the nicotine stained index fingernail. The systolic blood pressure was a little high but the diastolic was as good as a man much younger than what he appeared to be. However as I looked him in the face something in his eyes made my insides twist, and I began to feel sick.

Acting like I was calm, I smiled at him, patted his hand and asked him what he thought was the problem. He looked down and fiddled with his cigarette package before answering. He said he thought there was something wrong with his stomach. I asked him to elaborate. He then looked up and said he didn't think he should be discussing this with a young lady.

At this point the son came to stand beside him and said: "He's been having awful pain, nearly bent him in two. Do you have anything to help him with the pain?"

I stood up beside the younger man, looked directly at him and that something inside me sent me another warning. Walking away and back to the kitchen table I asked what sort of medication the father was on. Taking out the chart which Miss Brandt had given me I started recording the blood pressure. Then I remembered the internal warning I felt and zipped up my bag again. Continuing to ask questions, I began writing down what I observed, as well as the rather vague questionable answers they were giving to my questions. The young man came and stood beside me. He had started to perspire. He was also trembling a bit.

I sent a prayer: "Oh sweet Father, please help me! He's a drug addict!"

The dad got up smoothly and effortlessly from his easy chair, glided over to the table and said: "Lady, just give us the drugs in your bag. Can't you see he needs a painkiller more than me?" He smiled and those cold bare lips made me freeze to the spot.

"We don't carry medicine," I told them. "And if he needs something do you have any aspirin?" I was giving myself time to think and putting on what I thought was a composed front. They both laughed.

The young man went to the door and locked it. The older man leered at me hungrily again and my blood turned to ice.

I continued to talk and act calm. I think I asked the younger man about his symptoms all the while playing dumb to the truth of what was going on, and what might be going on soon. The older man kept squeezing closer to me, smiling that awful smile and rubbing against me. I stood up, distancing myself from him and started putting on my coat.

Out of nowhere came three loud bangs, then a final crash. "Open the door or I'll break it down!" a roaring voice ordered from outside the door. The two men froze. Then the young man went to the door and unlocked and opened it.

A fairly slim middle aged man of muscular build entered quickly and quietly. His large hazel eyes came quickly to me as he talked to the men. "So what are you up to now Cecil?"

I felt myself moving, even though I seemed rooted to the spot. I grabbed my bag. The younger man had unzipped it. Stuff fell out. Shakily I zipped it closed. I seemed to be moving in wobbly slow motion. "For God's sake speed up and get out of here," I commanded myself. I frantically finished putting my coat on, couldn't find the buttons, but started out.

The new man stopped me. "Oh Father, please help me," I prayed. That man smiled a real nice smile and said: "You're safe now, so please, just to wait a little." He asked me if the men were looking for drugs and I nodded my head. I felt frozen to the spot and for some reason I simply could not talk.

Turning back to the men he asked them: "Looking for drugs were you?" They seemed to know who he was.

He turned to me, asking gently, "Are you all right?" His face had turned kind, and his hazel eyes showed concern.

"I'm an RCMP officer. I've been watching these two and this place for days. They're drug addicts and dealers. We intercepted their supplier and they're both desperate as well as dangerous. Are you sure they didn't hurt you?"

I just looked at him and knew I had started to cry in relief. I couldn't speak. I was frozen and felt the tears flowing from my eyes. His hazel eyes looked at me in such a compassionate way and I knew I had started to sob in relief. He said: "When you went in and you weren't coming out I knew you were in trouble."

The RCMP officer pulled another kitchen chair over to me and pushed me gently by the shoulders to sit in it. He then questioned the men more, and when I felt a little better, he walked me out to my car. He told me that by going in after me he had blown his own cover, and it was useless now for him to remain, since he couldn't lay any charges. However, it was worth it to him to have saved me from something terrible.

I will be forever grateful to him for saving me and the tiny little baby growing inside me. God sent me an RCMP angel.

CHAPTER 27

Inside/Outside, a Last Tale of Spirit

"People say that what we're all seeking is a meaning for life.....I think that what we're seeking is an experience of being alive, so that our life experiences on the purely physical plane will have resonances within our own innermost being and reality, so that we actually feel the rapture of being alive...." - Joseph Campbell (The Power of Myth).

Hopefully, this last chapter will close off "A Tale of Spirit" in a very positive way. I'd like to think that in many ways we, the elders of society, teach by our lives and actions. The people in this chapter all live in the same senior park in Tucson called Desert Pueblo, some of us part time and others full time. We come from all over the United States and many of us also come from Canada, to enjoy Arizona's sunny winters. We've learned that growing older isn't a hindrance to living a fun filled life. Our band of musicians was asked to take part in a Senior Mardi Gras Night, and to give a band performance which will be described later, but first I want you to meet the band members.

We are a motley but interesting bunch. Our ages are all in the seventies or eighties bracket except for David who is still in his fifties.

Erwin Villiger and his wife Jackie lived for many years in Maryland. Originally Erwin is from Switzerland. He is retired, was a mechanical engineer. Erwin financed his university education by playing in bands, in Switzerland. He is tall, and somewhat lanky, with fair hair and blue eyes. Recently they discovered he had cancer in one lung and this was removed. He went right back to playing his saxophone.

Jackie is much shorter, with dark hair and eyes, and she is slim and athletic. She originally came from Caribou, Maine, and was a registered nurse. After Erwin and Jackie retired from their jobs they both toured the world in their sail boat, for three years. Their stories and experiences are exciting and remarkable. They followed the beauty of their dreams. Erwin plays soprano, alto and tenor saxophone and we talked his wife Jackie into playing maracas which she does very well. They have just settled down in our park recently, and have become permanent residents. Jackie has also taken up line dancing in our park.

William Platt (Curly) was a farmer from Ohio, as well as working in the general motors auto industry. He was stocky, broad shouldered and muscular, about five foot nine, with twinkling dark eyes and a shy smile. Curly got his nickname because of the magnificent head of curls he has had all his life. He loved his church and often sang solos in his beautiful bass voice. He learned to play the oboe in high school and later played in bands and orchestras. He had the greatest dry, sly sense of humor and always, at the most unexpected times, sent us all into stitches. Curly was very resourceful and could find solutions to anything. Prior to our presentation Curly had suffered a serious stroke and was recovering bravely but with difficulty. Although the stroke left him with severe memory impairment, and although his balance was a bit off, he managed to play and sing with us at practice mornings and also for the performance. When Curly went back to Ohio this year, he had another massive stroke and died. His warm and gentle spirit is loved by everyone and he will be greatly missed.

David Pauch was born totally blind with cataracts. It was also discovered that he was autistic.

He lived with his parents in Pennsylvania, went to a school for the blind, where he says, "they taught me how to get along despite having very little vision, and they also helped me lose some of my autism. Later as I grew older I lost some more autism." He received his first accordion at age eight, and in taking private lessons, his teachers discovered he had a real aptitude for music. When he was ten, his dad gave him a harmonica.

"It was a real harmonica, not the kind parents usually give to their kids" he mentioned with pride. David taught himself to play that harmonica and he plays it with great feeling. His mother plays piano, so David picked up that skill readily too. His parents were snowbirds travelling back and forth from Pennsylvania to Tucson until 1980 when David got a full time job in a music store in Tucson, whereupon the Pauch family then became full time residents in Desert Pueblo.

David and Curly were often a duo, David accompanying on accordion as Curly sang, giving their own performances at Coffee time on Saturday mornings. When David accompanies a soloist he does so with great sensitivity, and when he plays the jigs he so loves, the whole audience rocks. David is tall, quite lean, with a serious expression and a very determined jaw, earnest eyes, and a tight smile when he's happy.

Joyce and Bill Hodges are from Michigan. Joyce was a pre-kindergarten specialist and Bill, her husband worked in the used car business. Joyce has the kindest eyes when she talks to you, and her reddish hair and smile are captivating. She is the first to admit she is a little plump around her backside. (I tell you this because in the following story it is important that you remember this fact.) She moved slowly because of a recent hip replacement, but has picked up speed with recovery. She says "I get wherever I want to go". Joyce is our pianist and Bill our drummer.

Bill is slim, with laughing blue eyes and a good sense of humor. He was born with a cleft lip which was repaired surgically, but the scars remain, both visually and leaving him with a slight speech impediment. This certainly didn't hold him back in his work and doesn't to this day. He won many awards for sales in the used car company where he worked for over twenty years. Bill takes very good care of Joyce and she nicknamed him her "Sherpa."This is the second marriage for both of them. They were sweethearts as teenagers then drifted apart into different lives.   When both lost their first mates, and after a suitable wait, Bill came calling on Joyce and they got together again. Joyce plays piano well but wasn't used to the band music and Bill is now learning drums. They practice a great deal and are sounding like they've played in a band all their lives. They are a hoot together, and we have a great time with them. They are also a great example of the fact that we are never too old to learn new skills, and to be able to laugh at ourselves. They also plough through life's difficulties with determination, especially when things get tough.

I'm from Victoria, B.C. Canada, and play acoustic guitar, am learning electric bass guitar, play piano and percussion instruments. I'm short, about 4ft.11 and 1/2 am now a blonde, and have also been elected to be the band's female singer. I'm the band leader. My home originally was in Kirkland Lake, Ontario, Canada. Ray and I met while I was going to school. Both our mates had died. Ray calls himself the band's gopher, helping set up and take down the equipment and attending to off stage details. He also gives helpful critiques. We all appreciate Ray very much.

We had been practicing for the Mardi Gras celebration since January and having a great and sometimes hilarious time in practice. Part of the following chapter is from the actual script I wrote for the performance. The script counts on the vivid imaginations which we seniors have developed through the years. When the performance was on, the senior audience contributed right along with us.

So come along with us to The Senior Mardi Gras in Desert Pueblo, Tucson, Arizona.

We were the last to perform. The dancers had wowed the crowd, there were solos and joke tellers, and several performers before intermission. It was now our turn. We took our places on stage after Ray and a few others had assembled our equipment, chairs and music stands. There were six of us, Erwin on sax, Curly on oboe, David with his accordion and harmonica, Joyce on piano,

Bill on drums, and me with guitar and percussion sticks. Jackie had opted out because she was also a dancer in a previous number. Virginia Quarles introduced the numbers we were going to play in sets of three. Virginia is a much loved elegant lady who lives her life with wisdom and a good sense of humor. She was fabulous as our announcer. We hoped for audience participation so I adlibbed as we went along.

First the band was introduced, and I mentioned that we had lots of fun together, as well as being supportive of each other when difficulties like health issues hit us, explaining that both Curly and I had suffered strokes, Curly's severe and mine minor. (I did this to prepare the audience since I wasn't sure how many people knew of Curly's difficulty.) The audience learned how much David particularly had helped us, because he understood how to help people help themselves. (Most of the audience was familiar with the fact that David was legally blind but not all of them knew, since there were many new people.)

Once that was done the audience was asked if they were in the mood to have some fun. They looked back expectantly but no one volunteered an answer, so I asked again, louder this time, "Are you in the mood for some fun?" Some spoke up "yes", nodding their heads. Putting my hand to my ear, shaking my head I said loudly, "Can't hear you. Are you in the mood for some fun?" This time the audience boomed back, "Yes!"

Without another word the band broke into a loud "In the Mood". We played it several times and with the mike open the audience was invited to dance if they felt like it. One swinging couple got up to jitterbug.

Once the bouncing mood had been established, the lights were dimming and I spoke into the mike, "We are now flying over mountains and valleys on a magic carpet to Louisiana. Soon you will be sitting on an open, upper deck of a nightclub, sipping a margarita, and watching the people stroll by on the street below. The night is clear, the moon and stars shine brightly, and from someplace nearby you hear the soft strains of a harmonica."

David begins to play in the background, then comes forward

and plays into the mike the introduction to Summertime. He turns to me and in a low voice I sing. We are all taken "there" in New Orleans and wish there were more verses to that beautiful, well loved melody.

"Who has blue eyes? Put up your hands!" Several hands shoot up. "This song is for you so sit back, close your eyes and listen to Curly sing to you."David gives the intro on harmonica, the band takes up the music and Curly comes to the mike to sing in his beautiful bass voice, "Blue Spanish Eyes." The audience is enthralled and when invited, they joined in to sing too.

"Come on down to Louisiana's beach, put on your bathing suits, and as you are lounging on your towels someone very special is walking by. Yes, she is beautiful and can she ever wiggle! When feel like clapping to the beat, or maybe getting up to wiggle yourself, go right ahead!"

The band strikes up "Marianne" and the audience begins to clap along. (Before this number, Joyce, our pianist had put on around her waist a red triangular belly dancing scarf with many, many silver jingles in preparation for this number.) While the rest of the band is playing and really getting into it, Joyce slyly gets up, slides around the piano, sticks her round backside out to the audience and shakes it wildly to the beat. The jingles are amplified loud and clear. The audience takes a loud surprised intake of breath then breaks into hilarious laughter. They clap, stamp and shout " more, more more," but Joyce has disappeared back around the piano to pick up the beat and keep playing again. She has brought the house down. It takes awhile for all of us to stop laughing.

"Switzerland sends their favorite ambassador here, especially for this Mardi Gras. The problem is he can't remember the name of the song, so we've named it the "No Name Swiss Cheesy Waltz" Irwin plays a wonderful solo with David as back up on accordion and when they are finished the audience is invited to take part in the next medley to follow.

"If anyone feels like a nice quiet waltz, go ahead and dance, but be prepared for a change in tempo which will take you by surprise to

Kansas!" The band starts out dreamily playing a beautiful Viennese waltz, then follows it with the fast driving beat of "Kansas City" and the crowd beats right along with them every face smiling broadly. Towards the end I say "Let's keep right on strutting down to the darker part of town with Darktown Strutters Ball".

The dancers can't restrain themselves, getting up to dance they form a long line right around the room. They keep dancing, the music is loud and the room rocks. We keep playing three, four then five rounds. Finally I hold up my hand and say, "Maybe we had better slow down now or we might not get to sleep tonight. So let's reminisce a bit."

"This next song is a tribute to all us seniors who wear the gold medals of experience. We've had good times and hard times, laughed a lot, and cried a lot too, but we are the warriors of life and we've won most of our battles, because we're still here aren't we?" The audience roars, "Yes we're still here!"

"Then sing with us if you feel like it." The band plays the little known introduction gently, and then cuts into "When the Saints Come Marching In". With cheering and singing the audience joins us.

"The magic carpet has brought us back to Tucson. We need a lullaby to close our beautiful evening together. Here's Curly and David." Curly stands up shakily, with David putting a hand under his elbow. They approach the mike. David gives the intro and Curly's deep bass voice rings out strong and clear. "Old Man River, that old man river...." The audience is quiet, entranced. Then they begin to hum softly The humming sound is a deep magical background for Curly's superb voice.

We say goodnight to the people with reluctance. The audience gives all of us a standing ovation.

Senior Mardi Gras comes to a close with everyone remembering with warmth and love both the program and all our own past memories.

We all leave, as I too leave you, my readers, now, all of us remembering, and all of us "feeling the rapture of being alive".

Epilogue:

In the world of life and healing, another magic seems intertwined. People journey with us on our paths at different times when, it seems, we need them or they need us the most. I believe we all help each other and perhaps that's called an Essence of Spirit and part of the Magic.

My memories are my treasures. So many people have walked on my path and left their beautiful imprints of love in my heart. I say to them and to you all: "Thank you from and with my deepest Spirit."

I am aware and pass these torches of hope and love along to all of you. I want you to benefit from this book, A Tale of Spirit.

I also want to say to you, my granddaughter - Little Hope - that you have been wisely named. To you and to all the rest of my grandchildren and also my readers, I know that if you live your lives in a positive manner, hand in hand with your own Spirit, and know that your Spirit walks and talks with God, you will be spiritually wealthy beyond your dreams.

When you do this you will also be safe, will help humankind and will fulfill the jobs you came to do on this earth.

Namaste

LaVergne, TN USA
09 December 2010

207975LV00001B/2/P

Autism
Report Writing

Susan Louise Peterson